Explorations in Christology

American University Studies

Series VII
Theology and Religion

Vol. 37

PETER LANG
New York · Bern · Frankfurt am Main · Paris

John Anthony Sullivan

Explorations in Christology

The Impact of Process/Relational Thought

PETER LANG
New York · Bern · Frankfurt am Main · Paris

Library of Congress Cataloging-in-Publication Data

Sullivan, John Anthony
  Explorations in Christology.

  (American university studies. Series VII, Theology
and religion ; vol. 37)
  Bibliography: p.
  1. Jesus Christ—History of doctrines—20th century.
2. Process philosophy. 3. Process theology. I. Title.
II. Series: American university studies. Series VII,
Theology and religion ; v. 37.
BT198.S84 1987   232   87-2990
  ISBN 0-8204-0621-X
  ISSN 0740-0446

CIP-Kurztitelaufnahme der Deutschen Bibliothek

Sullivan, John Anthony:
Explorations in christology : the impact of
process / relational thought / John Anthony
Sullivan. – New York; Bern; Frankfurt am
Main; Paris: Lang, 1987
  (American University Studies: Ser. 7,
  Theology and Religion; Vol. 37)
  ISBN 0-8204-0621-X

NE: American University Studies / 07

© Peter Lang Publishing, Inc., New York 1987

Printed by Weihert-Druck GmbH, Darmstadt, West Germany

To M.W.M. -

Communicator of the graciousness of the Mystery, who positioned me to believe that "the incommunicable part of us is the pasture of God."

(Teilhard de Chardin)

TABLE OF CONTENTS

All scripture quotations used by the author are from *The New Oxford Annotated Bible with the Apocrypha* (Revised Standard Version), ed. by Herbert G. May and Bruce M. Metzger, 1977, New York: Oxford University Press.

PREFACE

The last part of the 20th century may someday be characterized as the "age of experience". The Scholastic and Neo-Platonic philosophy that shaped the theology of Aquinas and Augustine infiltrated theological reflection in the Christian tradition until the mid 1950's. Modernity correctly appreciated this formidable system of thought — and yet, due to the highly speculative metaphysical base of this theological construction, some religious thinkers experienced a certain "dis-ease" with this foundational approach because it did not appear to cohere with lived experience. The consequence was to search for a modern synthesis of thought that reflected the contemporary consciousness of lived reality and, at the same time, did justice to the long tradition of creedal and definitional characteristics of the Christian faith rooted in the Scriptural testimony.

The Process/Relational thought of Alfred North Whitehead and Charles Hartshorne entered my conceptual horizon in the early 1970's due to research in preparation for an undergraduate course entitled "Introduction to Theology". It fascinated and intrigued me because it "backed into" theism from the world of the mathematical and natural sciences. In truth, it was only a casual and superficial understanding because the complexity and strangeness of vocabulary in the seminal thinkers (Whitehead and Hartshorne) had not been investigated in extensive depth — and so many Roman Catholic theologians saw it as an esoteric school of Christian discourse that was even "suspect". Nevertheless, interest in Process/Relational thought continued and was eventually fueled by a course in Graduate School entitled "Directions in Contemporary Theology".

It must be stated initially that Process/Relational philosophy and theology is a very diverse school of thought. Inconsistencies and misunderstandings abound — as this project will aptly demonstrate. Even Charles Hartshorne, the primary disciple of Alfred North Whitehead, developed some key process concepts that I'm sure Whitehead himself never would have envisaged! Thus, a process theologian who has Scholasticism as a background will filter his experience of reality, God, and Christ in a different fashion than a process thinker who has Heidegger or Hegel as a philosophical context. Even so, it is my contention that Process/Relational philosophy and theology is a particularly effective tool to express the Christian faith to 20th century Americans!

Part I of my thesis presentation will treat basically of four concepts:

1) events — not things — are the basis of reality;
2) all of reality is inter-related; and identity is an emergent from relationship;
3) the goal or intentionality of process is creative advance or creative transformation, i.e. towards the "more" or self-transcendence; and
4) the bi-polarity of the God of process theology; the primordial character of God whereby he touches humanity and history through the possibilities he offers, and the consequent nature of God whereby humanity and history actually have an impact on God.

Part II will then attempt to apply these "neo-classical theistic" concepts to the manner in which (with consistency) the image of Christ must be re-appropriated or re-configurated. W. Norman Pittenger and John B. Cobb, Jr., have been selected to theorize on the nature or event of Christ in relation to God and the human and cosmic enterprise.

Part III will struggle to correlate Cobb's "image" of the Christ as creative transformation with Paul Tillich's existentialist ontological conceptualization of Christ as the bearer of "New Being". The impetus for the introduction of Tillich into a project on Process Theology comes from Cobb himself in his book **Christ in a Pluralistic Age.** In their realization of theological pluralism and their desire for a broad ecumenicity, Cobb and Tillich portray their "images" or "symbols" of the Christ as exclusive of arrogant particularity.

Part IV will propose my own critique of both Cobb and Tillich, and attempt to demonstrate through selected citations their complementarity, even though their foundational metaphysical base is quite diverse.

Neither process cosmology nor existential ontology will be painted with finality. Both have their limitations — as does any philosophico-theological system. Straight "God-talk" must move into metaphor; then into poetry; and then into muteness in the presence of Godly mystery!

The basic theological objective of my presentation is to demonstrate that these two modalities of doing theology and christology are *not* mutually exclusive. There does seem to be *some* congeniality in both systems when the conversation turns to actual, concrete predicates about God; when "atonement theology" speaks of the *factual* suffering of God in Christ; and especially when the concept of "presence" and "symbol" ("image" or "focus") is interpreted to be an *event* that discloses a fuller reality than itself and really participates in what it discloses ("Being Itself").

It has often been said that creativity is the art of forgetting the sources of one's ideas. While I have tried to acknowledge the sources of my ideas when I am conscious of them, I am sure that in many cases I have been negligent, and forgetfulness alone accounts for *apparent* creativity. Therefore, I ask the indulgence of my *more professional* colleagues in process theology; and I ask the reader to take seriously the fact that this book is heavily indebted not only to the volumes and articles listed in the bibliography, but to a host of readings, lectures and conversations.

I must extend my immense gratitude to my mentors and friends, Dr. Larry Folkemer and Dr. Gerald Christianson of the Lutheran Theological Seminary at Gettysburg; to Monsignor Carroll E. Satterfield, S.T.D., of the College of Notre Dame in Baltimore; to Dr. William Collinge and Dr. William Portier, chairman and seer, respectively, of the College Theology Department at Mount Saint Mary's in Emmitsburg, Maryland; to Fathers Steve Feehan and Frank DiDomenico, professors at the Seton Hall University Graduate School of Theology, South Orange, N.J.; to Father Bernard J. Lee, S.M., inspirational lecturer on process themes; to Charles V. Gearhart, Director of Printing Services at Mount Saint Mary's College; to Yvonne Wickenheiser, patient secretary and masterful corrections-maker; to the courteous and expert personnel of the libraries at the Lutheran Theological Seminary in Gettysburg and at Mount Saint Mary's College; to Jay Wilson, Editor-in-Chief of Peter Lang Publishing, Inc., who took a chance on this "rookie", and to Monsignor Vincent Molloy, S.T.D., theological companion at Mount Saint Mary's College, who helped to streamline and sanitize the text.

May the mysterious God of Jesus and his companions hold them precious in his memory!

I. INTRODUCTION

In the book of Exodus (34:6), the Lord is described as "a God merciful and gracious, slow to anger, and abounding in steadfast love and faithfulness." When Israel is so turned away from the Lord that she is unwilling, even incapable, of returning to the covenantal relationship, God so wills that relationship that he is converted to a new way: "My heart recoils within me, my compassion grows warm and tender. I will not execute my fierce anger, I will not again destroy Ephraim" (Hosea 11:8).

In Amos 7:3, 6, a similar note is sounded. Amos prays to the Lord on behalf of Israel, interceding that he not act in his justifiable wrath against Israel. And God is stirred by the prayer: "The Lord repented concerning this; 'It shall not be', said the Lord." A parallel narrative is found in the book of Jonah 3:10: "When God saw what they did, how they turned from their evil way, God repented of the evil which he had said he would do to them; and he did not do it." And in the Book of Proverbs 8:30-31, the personification of Wisdom recites: "Then I was beside him, like a master workman (or little child); and I was daily his delight, rejoicing before him always, rejoicing in his inhabited world and delighting in the sons of men."

Walter Brueggemann asserts that "there is no more radical idea than this in the entire Bible. God is presented not primarily as all-knowing, all-powerful, or all-present but as a covenant partner who freely makes intervention and fresh decision toward his covenant partner . . . He is not a static object or a passive entity, but, on the contrary, he is a dynamic covenant partner who in his faithful compassion can act in various ways to renew and transform. The radical announcement of the Bible is that God himself is converted on behalf of his people . . . His 'godness' consists not in remote indifference but in passionate freedom to sustain his relation with his people."[1]

The Psalmist presupposes continuously that his Lord is a God of passionality and feeling. Two citations will suffice to demonstrate that the Hebrew God is not a Lord of unaffectability. The Psalmist asks in 77:7-9: "Will the Lord spurn for ever, and never again be favorable? Has his steadfast love for ever ceased? Are his promises at an end for all time? Has God forgotten to be gracious?'' And Psalm 103:13 (attributed to David) has the Psalmist speak of an emotional God: "As a father pities his children, so the Lord pities those who fear him.''

The sociologist-theologian-columnist-novelist Andrew Greeley comments that "in the Hebrew scriptures there are many pleas to Yahweh that he come down and be appeased, that he forgive his poor, stupid, offending people instead of rampaging around the cedars of Lebanon tearing things up in his fury . . . While the other gods stood aloof on their mountaintops waiting for the people to come to them, Yahweh came down off the mountain and intervened directly in human affairs. He announced peremptorily, 'I am Yahweh your God' . . . our experience of God in the Yahwistic tradition is one of non-abandoning love.''[2]

The Christian Scriptures speak of the Lord as a benevolent God of love who sent his only Son that humankind might live in a world of love, joy, and peace. For example, in the Gospel of Luke 6:35-36: "Love your enemies, and do good, and lend, expecting nothing in return; and your reward will be great, and you will be sons of the Most High; for he is kind to the ungrateful and the selfish. Be merciful, even as your Father is merciful.'' The author of the Fourth Gospel (3:16) claims that "God so loved the world that he gave his only Son, that whoever believes in him should not perish but have eternal life.'' And the Johannine Epistles are highlighted in 1 John 4:8-11 where the author attests that "he who does not love does not know God; for God is love. In this the love of God was made manifest among us, that God sent his only Son into the world, so that we might live through him. In this is love, not that we loved God but that he loved us and sent his Son to be the expiation for our sins. Beloved, if God so loved us, we also ought to love one another.''

Even in the earlier Pauline corpus, we can find the appalled Paul writing to the troublesome Galatians (2:20): "I have been crucified with Christ; it is no longer I who live, but Christ who lives in me; and the life I now live in the flesh I live by faith in the Son of God, who loved me and gave himself for me.'' For our purposes, perhaps the most important Pauline text would be from II Corinthians 5:17-21: "Therefore, if any one is in Christ, he is a new creation; the old has passed away, behold, the new has come. All this is from God, who through Christ reconciled us to himself and gave us the ministry of reconciliation; that is, God was in Christ reconciling the world to himself, not counting their trespasses against them, and entrusting to us the message of reconciliation. So we are ambassadors for Christ, God making his appeal through us. We beseech you on behalf of Christ, be reconciled to God. For our sake he made him to be sin who knew no sin, so that in him we might become the righteousness of God."

A problem surfaces when one tries to reconcile such scriptural language with the philosophical proclamation that God is "unchangeable" and "unaffected." Greek philosophers developed a notion of God which insisted upon his self-consistency: he never suffered passion or feeling. God was impassible (*apathes*). His will was determined from *within* instead of being swayed from *without*. This concept of God as perfect, impassible, unmoved and unmovable influenced Christian writers: the early Church Fathers, Aquinas, and subsequent generations of Christian theologians. For example, Plato and Aristotle both held to the concept of the Unmoved Mover. And in his "Magna Moralia," Aristotle takes his view of the unchanging deity to its logical conclusion. He claims that God is so unchangeable that he cannot love us and we cannot in any way love him for that would involve movement. "In the Magna Moralia, Aristotle says expressly that those are wrong who think that there can be friendship towards God. For (a) God could not return our love, and (b) we could not in any case be said to love God."[3] The God of Aristotle, therefore, cannot be a provident God. He does not know nor love anything other than himself. He is an eternal act of self-consciousness which eternally thinks itself and nothing else.

If this is true, modern people are tempted to ask how such notions of God allow for his love to respond to their prayer. For example, in the Roman Catholic ascetical and liturgical tradition, there have been numerous "litanies" that implore the mercy of God. In the context of the Eucharist or Lord's Supper, after the liturgy of the

Word and just prior to the liturgy of the Eucharist, there is a section entitled "General Intercessions" or the "Prayer of the Faithful." The directions of the Sacramentary describe this as a time when "as a priestly people we unite with one another to pray for today's needs in the Church and the world." The most frequent optional response to these General Intercessions is "Lord, hear our prayer." Votive Masses "for the sick," "for peace and justice," "for any need," "for ministers and vocations," "for unity of Christians," for almost any need imaginable have been celebrated over the century. It is extremely difficult to consider that these exhortations really make a difference to God and affect human history and persons if qualities such as love and compassion cannot be compatible with a self-sufficient infinite reality who possesses all he needs from all eternity and can never become, because he is already pure being. Therefore, he cannot sympathize; he cannot really act in human history.

For this reason, Daniel Dugan can maintain that "the 'I love you' addressed to mankind by a God who remained totally invulnerable would be shallow and ineffectual . . . if God's love for men had as its only purpose their adoration of him, it would not be genuine love."[4] In this concept of an immutable and impassible God, God might appear to be dangerously without present employment![5] The reason for this is that most of our theological reflection has been done in terms of the primacy of changeless being. In this school of thought, God is defined as being *par excellence*, the Supreme Being in whom no change is possible because it would imply imperfection. No one changes unless there is something to be gained by it. Since God is perfect, it would seem inappropriate to think of him as changing. Whatever existence means for God, it seems not to involve any kind of change.

While it is true that God represents all that is perfect and sublime, there is nothing in his nature to prevent him from seeking to express his infinite goodness in finite ways. In fact, that is what creation is all about — God seeking to express his infinite perfection in finite ways. Whereas finite things change in order to become more perfect, God changes so as to manifest his perfection in every way possible, even to the point of taking on flesh and becoming human.

Scripture is replete with references that suggest God adapts himself to changing conditions in the world and accommodates himself to specific human needs. None is more dramatic than the belief that God has become incarnate and entered history in his fullness. We attest to this belief each time we proclaim the Christian creed formulated in the earliest days of the Church. The Nicean Creed expressly declares that God *became* man. In explicating the Trinitarian life of God, we speak of the Son *proceeding* from the Father. Both indicate some kind of becoming or process in God. ⌐

One of the best scriptural descriptions of divine becoming appears in the Letter to the Philippians 2:6-7. There the Apostle Paul says of Christ Jesus that "his state was divine, yet he did not cling to his equality with God but emptied himself to assume the condition of a slave, and became as men are." The passage suggests that in Jesus the divine nature reaches out beyond itself to assume the condition of humanity, not standing on prerogative or privilege, but leaving behind the perfection of divinity to become like us in all things except sin.

God is never called impassible in the Christian Scriptures. The letters of Ignatius of Antioch employ the term for the first time; in his Epistle to Polycarp 3:2 and Ephesians 7:2 the term is applied to the divinity of Christ, and in Malachi 3:6 and James 1:17 he attributed immutability to God. Justin Martyr in the second century adopted a Middle Platonist philosophical idea of God and a world view that were an eclectic amalgam of Platonism and Aristotelianism — and after Justin the notion of impassibility becomes a standard part of the Christian vocabulary. Robert M. Grant notes that the adoption of this attribute for God is paralleled by relatively few references to God's benevolence in the subsequent writings of early Christians, especially in comparison with the Scriptural witness.[6]

The question that must be clarified is this: whether impassibility must be considered an essential and irrevocable attribute of the God of the Christians? It should be noted here that the early Church Fathers were always struggling with the tensions between their philosophical, unchanging God and the biblical, passionate God. This is true from Justin Martyr to Anselm of the twelfth century, who is the gateway from the patristic era into the age of

Scholasticism. Anselm, in fact, even addresses himself to God concerning this problem: "But how are You at once both merciful and impassible? For if You are impassible You do not have any compassion; and if You have no compassion Your heart is not sorrowful from compassion with the sorrowful, which is what being merciful is . . . Therefore You are both merciful because You save the sorrowful and pardon sinners against You; and You are not merciful because You do not experience any feeling of compassion for misery."[7]

Like Job in the Hebrew Scriptures, the most popular contemporary expression of this tension in faith might well be the bestseller "When Bad Things Happen to Good People" written by Rabbi Harold S. Kushner. In his analysis of the story of Job, Kushner asks: "Is God saying, as some commentators suggest, that He has other considerations to worry about, besides the welfare of one individual human being, when He makes decisions that affect our lives? Is He saying that, from our vantage point, our sicknesses and business failures are the most important things imaginable, but God has more on his mind than that? To say that is to say that the morality of the Bible, with its stress on human virtue and the sanctity of the individual life, is irrelevant to God, and that charity, justice, and the dignity of the individual human being have some source other than God. If that were true, many of us would be tempted to leave God, and seek out and worship that source of charity, justice, and human dignity instead."[8]

Professor Joachim Jeremias has a bold and exciting suggestion concerning Matthew 24:42-44 and Luke 12:39-40. He writes that "Jesus does not regard the will of God as fixed or immutable. God can shorten the days for the sake of the elect (Luke 18:7-8), and he can lengthen the period of grace (Luke 13:6-9) as a free act of mercy."[9] It is due to the grace and mercy of God that the end did not come when Jesus said it would, but God has given humankind a longer time to prepare for the great day.

Likewise, when Jesus prayed "The Lord's Prayer" (Luke 11:1-4; cf. Matthew 6:9-13), he used the word *Abba* (instead of the formal and exclusively religious *Abinu*) with which a child addressed his/her father. Jesus, it seems, transformed the Fatherhood of God from a theological doctrine into an intense and intimate experience. Even the non-Christian Juvenal said on one occasion: "Dearer is a man to the gods than to himself."

II. PROCESS THOUGHT

Modernity has gradually displaced the notion of the universe as inherited from Greek philosophy. A powerful new foundational theological construction has emerged from England and North America called "Process Theology." The process thought of Alfred North Whitehead (d. 1947) is "a very complicated system of thought . . . The recent, almost inordinate, popularity of 'process thought' in Catholic educational circles suggests that complexity is no obstacle. If the truth be told, it is only the *general notion* of process rather than the actual body of process philosophy which has been appropriated and applied."[10] The world was at one time viewed as "the world of Isaac Newton, which is to say, a world of fixed, immutable laws. Our planet was seen to be a vast complex machine, pre-wound and sliding into position, as it were, according to very fixed and discoverable laws of nature. An immobile God for a clockwork world was compatible enough."[11]

But "Newton's insights regarding gravity and the tendency of bodies to stay in motion eliminated the need for Aristotle's First Mover who, as a Final Cause, effected the circular motion of the intelligent outermost sphere. Darwin's theory of evolution established the idea the the world is not static but enjoys a process of growth into greater perfection. After Einstein the ultimate foundation of physical reality is seen to involve relationships. Because the very worldviews which originally excluded any possible relationship with God have all but disappeared, some new options are possible in talking about God. To speak of him as love is to define him by his personal relationships. He transcends in his relationships and not by any absolute exclusion of them."[12] Theology is incurably cultural, i.e., it always tries to utilize the best intellectual and emotional tools of its time. If Thomas Aquinas were living today, he might or might not be a process theologian. But he certainly wouldn't be an unreconstructible Thomist!

Although Karl Rahner's philosophical presuppositions are different from those of process thinkers, his ideas on "God becoming" in the Incarnation have a Whiteheadian tonality. When he asks what the meaning is of the assertion that "the Word of God has *become* man," he confronts the very same theological problematic which troubled the early Fathers. Rahner writes, for example, that "the acknowledgement of the unchanging and unchangeable God in his eternally perfect fullness is not merely a postulate of philosophy, it is also a dogma of faith. Nonetheless, it remains true the Word *became* flesh."[13]

Rahner has always recognized the fact of Incarnation as the fundamental dogma of Christianity. Consequently, he feels compelled to say: "God can become something; he who is unchangeable in himself can *himself* become subject to change in something else."[14] For Rahner, the revelation of "God's becoming" in the Incarnation brings us to an ontological ultimate which a purely rational ontology may not even suspect or may find difficult to accept. Some process theologians have attempted to adopt Rahner into their family because of his insights mentioned above — and Rahner's 'dynamist' ontology of human knowing and being does have some resemblance to certain process predispositions. "However," writes Robert Kress, "the inclusion of Rahner among process theologians would stretch the term beyond recognition. In any case, process theologians will generally find Rahner too much of a classical metaphysician."[15]

Process theology is a multi-faceted and rather radical proposal that challenges the traditional classical theistic ways of speaking about God and bases itself on unique philosophical premises. It is one of many attempts of our time to create greater coherence between the understanding of our experience of God and our understanding of the world in which we live — always with the awareness and within the framework that God is always going to be beyond our human conceptualizations and symbols which will need new conceptual formulations and symbolic expressions in the future. Process theology is predicated upon the cosmology of Alfred North Whitehead and takes seriously his famous injunction that "religion requires a metaphysical backing; for its authority is endangered by the intensity of the emotions which it generates."[16] Perhaps "process theology" is not even the best title for this rather diverse enterprise. The emphasis in this framework of thought is really on relationality, the organicness of the world, and the constitutionality between the relationship of God and the world. This philosophy has been baptized as "process" due to the title of Whitehead's *magnum opus* "Process and Reality" (1929). The term "process" rightly suggests that this movement rejects static actuality and affirms that all actuality is process.

Charles Hartshorne is the chief spokesperson for this viewpoint. Drawing primarily though not exclusively upon the philosophy of Alfred North Whitehead (1861-1947), he argues that "God must be thought of more dynamically and in a way more consistent with a social conception of reality. Rather than suppose that God is 'above it all' and totally unaffected by what is going on in the world, we should presume that God is the most affected being in the universe, the one who experiences everything. Such a one might still be thought of as absolute, though not in the traditional sense of being totally self-sufficient but as needing no particular thing in order to be who he is. Hartshorne calls his viewpoint 'panentheism' to distinguish it from 'theism,' which puts God wholly outside the world, and from 'pantheism,' which identifies God with the world."[17]

Whitehead and Hartshorne themselves have identified their distinctive contributions with other terms. Whitehead spoke of his thought as the "philosophy of organism" to point to his understanding of the individuals of which the world is composed. Hartshorne has spoken of "societal realism" to stress that there is a plurality of real entities intimately related. He has also used the term "creative synthesis" to emphasize that each entity is a self-creation out of a complex many. When Hartshorne describes his position on God, he has called himself a "neo-classical theist" to indicate his relation of continuity and discontinuity with traditional and classical theism, a "di-polar theist" to accentuate his critique of the one-sidedness of traditional theism, and a "panentheist" to indicate his view of the relation of God and the world.

Process theology, of course, speaks about God. Whitehead and Hartshorne have both used the word "God" frequently and without embarrassment. However, they have been conscious that what they have meant by the term is philosophically and religiously opposed to much that has been meant by "God" in metaphysical, theological, and popular traditions.

Process theology denies the existence of the Hellenic concept of God, which maintained that "perfection" entailed complete immutability or lack of change. That notion of impassibility stressed that deity must be completely unaffected by any other reality and must lack all passion or emotional response. This notion that deity is the "Absolute" has meant that God is not really related to the world and that God is wholly independent of the world, i.e., the God-world relation is purely *external* to God. In brief, the world contributes nothing to God, and God's influence upon the world is in no way conditioned by divine responsiveness to unforeseen, self-determining activities of worldly beings. For process theologians, this concept of the divine must collapse if "God" is to have any coherence with the immediacy of lived experience and the biblical witness. The philosophical presupposition of process modes of thought is that "becoming" is normative; "becoming" is the story of every reality; where there is no "becoming," there is not anything presently real. "Becoming" is not only not an imperfection, it is the very condition of being actual. Process is reality. The question of God's presence to creation is a question of how he acts, i.e., how he affects the course of creative advance.

As we shall attempt to see, Hartshorne and Whitehead have provoked Christian theologians in contemporary Western culture to ask an understanding of humankind's relationship with God in a way which makes sense in our world. Contemporary people are acutely aware of the strict limitations of their ability to probe behind "the supernatural scenes" and see the inner workings of the divine mind and will by which God produces his results. In ancient times, scholars thought they could do that. Such abilities that modern Christian theoreticians do possess to probe the things of God should be employed "in order to answer the religious question our contemporaries really care about: 'What does it mean to talk of God . . . in a world which is, so to speak, infinite both in space and time, in which all scientific events are interrelated in what seems to be an unbroken web, and in which all historical events are interrelated in what seems to us to be an unbroken web of motivation and causation?' In *this* world, the world of *our* culture, what does it mean to speak of God, and in particular what does it mean to talk of God acting in and toward this world, intervening in it? In the modern world, as David Freidrich Strauss put it, in a typically caustic phrase, 'a housing problem has arisen for God' . . . This is where our energies need to be directed. How are we to knit up the relationship to God which we have inherited, treasured and tried to deepen in the Christian tradition, with the insights which we also inevitably have as members of advanced Western technological society."[18]

Theologizing is a reflection on the faith. Christian theology has always had a penchant for reflecting theologically in very close rapport with philosophical categories of thought. Certainly in the last thirty years much of the thought that has been employed in order to attempt to explore the dwelling place of Christian faith has been done in the framework of process thought. As mentioned previously, the main person in our time to spearhead the notion of process thinking was Alfred North Whitehead of England. A scientist and mathematician, he eventually developed a philosophy of science on the nature of reality based on the tender elements in the world which slowly and in quietness operate by love.[19]

Love, which neither rules (the ancient monarchial model of God) nor is unmoved (the classical deistic model) became the starting point for Whitehead's theistic philosophy, i.e., it is precisely love which must be perfect in God. Whitehead could not think of God without relating him to a world in which his created goodness is concretized. Modernity should find this a very attractive and coherent concept of God, not only because we see the God of Scripture shift from a warrior God to a God of love, but also because the major creative expressions today in the areas of literature, psychology, philosophy and sociology insist upon the understanding of the self as relative. We are authentic selves only in direct proportion to our ability to be affected by and related to other selves. In brief, we are profoundly *relative* not substantial beings. Whether we know it or not, we are the persons we are because this certain idea has taken hold of us, this certain friend has literally entered our lives, this certain set of historical experiences has affected us.

In fact, the most human and the most religious of all experiences is by definition a relative concept, i.e., the experience of love. The experience of love is a manifestation of our innate demand for relatedness to others. Is it then possible to affirm today with the ordinary understanding of classical Christian theology that God alone is in no real way affected by others? Is it possible to affirm that God precisely as God "affects" but is not really affected by our lives? For the experience of love not only signals our innate need for relatedness to others, but also means that the more profoundly we love someone the more completely we are really *shaped* by that love relationship.

Whitehead would contend that a credible and real God for modernity would be both absolute (as the one whose *existence* depends on no other being) and relative (as the one whose *actuality* is relative to all other beings.) Whitehead's God, therefore, is dipolar, having a primordial and a consequent nature. He comments that God "viewed as primordial, is the unlimited conceptual realization of the absolute wealth of potentiality."[20] And "his unity of conceptual operations is a free creative act, untrammelled by reference to any particular course of things."[21] The particularities of the actual world presuppose the primordial nature of God — and the nature of God merely presupposes the *general* metaphysical character of creative advance, of which it is the primordial exemplification.

The primordial side of God's nature — his "design" (logos) — is free, complete, and eternal but *actually* deficient and unconscious. The consequent nature of God is determined, incomplete, "everlasting," fully actual, and conscious.[22] It originates with physical experience derived from the temporal, and then acquires integration with the primordial side. God becomes actualized with the concrescence of the world becoming.[23] By reason of the relationality of all things, the world affects God as he receives it into his experience. "Concrescence" is Whitehead's word for a particular act of becoming. It is the "on-going" or becoming stage of "a growing together," a creation of a unity out of a many.

No group better appreciates and explains the ongoing nature of creation than process theologians. For them, creation is a daily occurrence in which God opens up each new moment to possibilities for growth and originality that go beyond what creatures can do on their own. Without the creative activity of God, the world would soon run out of steam, living out its past until it had nothing left. With God as its creator, the world always has before it new horizons and limitless possibilities for life in abundance.

With its emphasis on creation as a current event, process theology goes so far as to reject the idea that the finite universe had an absolute beginning in time. The idea of a point before creation when God was all alone makes no sense in a universe of process. It is strictly a carryover from a world view that tries to explain things in terms of "why being, rather than non-being." If that is the way one formulates the problem, then God is a likely answer. It just so happens that for process theologians the question of being or not being is no longer pressing, or even legitimate. If asked at all, it must be answered in terms of becoming.

To interpret creation as making something out of nothing is to liken God to a super prestidigatator who makes things appear out of air so thin it is non-existent. To avoid that odious comparison, process theologians drop the imagery of making something out of nothing and see God rather as a life-giving wellspring that will never run dry for a universe that had always existed and always will exist in some form or other. In a process perspective, the world is everlasting because there never was a point at which God was not or will not be creating.

If creation were an after-thought on God's part, it would put him in the unenviable position of being a procrastinator. Being eternal himself, there is no earthly or heavenly reason why he could not and should not originate, sustain and fulfill a universe with no beginning or end in time. A God who chose not to create until he was good and ready would be less generous and loving than a God who shares his goodness with creatures from all eternity. It is hard to imagine what might cause him to wait or what could finally prompt him to act that was not part of his nature from the beginning.

The difference between God and us is not that he creates and we do not. The difference is that he creates from all eternity, while our power to create is finite and limited. Unlike the medieval conception where God alone was thought to create, process theology recognizes that this special gift has been passed on to us as well. We too participate in the making of this world by being co-creators with God. To be creative means to do more with life than simply repeat old-fashioned patterns. It means tying together the loose ends of history in a fresh and more profound synthesis. It means being able to cope with the increasing complexities of each successive generation and making of them the ingredients for a new arrangement of life.

Above all, it means assuming responsibility for our own future and that of others by joining with God in the creation of self and community. Our personal creation did not begin and end with the infusion of a soul at the moment of conception. It is part and parcel of life as a whole and we are its agents in conjunction with God.

For the process thinker, everything is inextricably tied up and connected with everything else, so that a change in the meaning of divine creation has repercussions on all other attributes of God. An especially important one is the matter of God's freedom. If God is always creating, as these theologians maintain, then his freedom no longer seems to involve the question of whether or not to create. Creation is a foregone conclusion for a God who has been doing it from time immemorial. The thought of not doing it would never have occurred to him.

The process view of creation does not allow for a supposed period of delay during which God could have pondered the possibility of leaving nothing be. God's freedom is not a matter of saying "yes" or "no" to creation. He always says "yes" to whatever possibilities there are for good, even finite ones like creation. This is what Paul must have been driving at when he wrote in his Second Letter to the Corinthians 1:19: "Jesus Christ, whom Silvanus, Timothy and I preached to you as Son of God, was not alternatively 'yes' or 'no'; he was never anything but 'yes'."

In the act of creation, God is eminently free, even though saying "no" is not part of his nature. This is because the kind of freedom exercised by God does not involve choice. The ability to choose is a finite form of freedom whereby an individual, because limited, must pick one option and deliberately exclude others. In the case of God, no such limitation exists. God acts on everything he possibly can; the idea of his saying "no" goes against the grain. Neither does

God play favorites, as we are told in Acts 10:34: "The truth I have now come to realize is that God does not have favorites, but that anybody of any nationality who fears God and does what is right is acceptable to him." God gives of himself whole and entire to everything and everyone. He cannot help but be all things to all creatures. That is his nature as an all-good and powerful God. To do less would be a violation of his true self and an act of personal infidelity, alternatives obviously not congruent with God.

Because God is necessary in himself, there is some degree of necessity in how he acts. He always acts in the best way possible and never hesitates to do what he can. If creation is a possibility for God, it is also a necessity, because he does everything he possibly can. In God, possibility and actuality are one, so that whatever he can do, he does. If the world falls short of being the best possible, the fault lies not with a recalcitrant God, but with obstinate creatures who rarely choose the best and all too frequently prefer the sinful.

The idea that true freedom does not necessarily involve real choice is not original with process theologians. As far back as the fourth century, Augustine distinguished between freedom (*libertas*) and free choice (*liberum arbitrium*) to show that the choosing of sin actually results in the diminution of real freedom. Thomas Aquinas in the thirteenth century had a similar insight at the other end of the spectrum when he maintained that in the beatific vision the human person cannot help but freely respond to God. "But the will of man who sees God in his essence of necessity adheres to God, just as now we desire of necessity to be happy." (Summa Theologiae I, Q. 82, Art. 2)

There is a deep mystery in such an expression as "cannot help but freely act" because it conjoins two qualities that are usually considered incompatible, namely, freedom and necessity. Yet, it is part of tradition to believe that we creatures will experience the reconciliation of both in the moment of final truth when God is seen face to face. Unfortunately, process thought does not envision such a moment in human experience, but it does define God as the reconciliation of opposites, the one in whom becoming and being, time and eternity, unity and plurality, identity and relationship find their common ground and perfect balance. Included in this reconciliation is the apparent incompatibility between freedom and necessity. In whatever God does, he is freely necessary and necessarily free. His act of creation is no exception to the rule.

This concept of a dipolar God may sound strange to classical theistic minds. But, this dipolarity in God becomes less difficult to grasp, many process thinkers urge, if we consider first not God's but our own analogously dipolar structure. For in one aspect of our personhood — that highly abstract aspect whereby we simply *exist* — we are not affected by others. We simply exist. Yet, in another aspect of our reality, our actual, concrete person, we are intrinsically and deeply *related* to others. As a feeling, thinking, willing, acting self, we are related to our own bodies (as our first environment), to other persons, to our historical moment, to such other historical moments as we can appropriate, etc. In a word, we are ourselves dipolar. As merely existing, we are relatively unrelated to others. As this concrete person (our "actuality"), we are through and through a relative creature.

Whitehead sees the universe as pluralist; its elements are not independent but related. It consists of an infinite and related number of occasions for becoming, each of which draws on being in a process which is the endless realization of potentialities.[24] Every individual reality is a potentiality for *being* an element in a new synthesis of endless *becoming*. The already actual can always become new when it moves toward a goal. However, one must be careful not to simply identify the world with becoming and flux, and God with being and permanence.[25] [N.B. Process is not to be identified with progress. Any process theologian who slides over the disturbing ambiguities and serious limitations of our actual situation expressed by the existentialists does a disservice to the contribution of Whitehead.]

The world, in other words, might protect its being, the present *status quo*, unless it were lured toward concretizing a new subject and ideal by an underlying energy of realization which is Creativity. As the "lure for feeling, the eternal urge of desire," God is the source of becoming who overcomes the world's compulsion with the static present by the persuasive lure of what might be.[26] God's activity in the world is always and only persuasive, never coercive. The full coercion of subjectivity is incompatible with freedom, and freedom resides in the character of the real. God *cannot* coerce decisions. Instead, he acts by attraction, i.e., he lures with the possibilities of value he holds out for the creative becoming of the world.

Process theologians believe in miracles, but not the kind that presume God acts on the world by occasionally intervening from the outside. God is fully implicated in history, and everything that happens is a sign of his power (and its limits, as well). God does not interrupt or contravene the natural course of events which he himself put in place. What he does is offer the world new opportunities for dealing with its problems and developing its potential. God does not do things, so much as give us himself that we might be more ourselves. He comes as one who offers hope for the future, not as one dispensing ready-made gifts and solutions.

The power of God is such that, while infinite in itself, it has limits when it operates in history. God is not a power baron who manipulates events so that everything will work out according to plan. That kind of power is unworthy of God and actually a sign of weakness. It is the kind of power exercised in the political arena by those who are profoundly insecure and have to control every detail lest something go wrong and their power base begin to crumble.

Unlike political bigwigs, God is the kind of leader who shares his power with others. It is a mistake to think that all things are in God's hands. That was the case primordially, in the sense that all power comes from God. He has in fact freely surrendered his monopoly on power and selflessly gives us much of it to act as we see fit. If the world is not as good as it can be, the fault is ours, not God's. We have failed to exercise properly the power God entrusted to us.

God is so great that he shares his power with others, knowing full well that it may be turned against him. God can countenance opposition, face rejection, have his particular preferences contravened, and still be strong enough to "keep things going." (Here it would be better to say "win out in the end," but process thought does not envision an end-time.) God does not win every encounter with humans and nature or there would be no sin. This much we can say with assurance: though evil may predominate in any given age, it will never completely triumph. God's power is too much for that to happen.

According to Whitehead, "the consequent nature of God is the fluent world become everlasting by its objective immortality in God."[27] God offers the world permanence in the primordial unity of his vision and derives his flux from the world. Neither God nor the world reaches static completion. Whitehead presupposes that both are in the grip of the ultimate metaphysical ground, the creative advance into novelty. God and the world are the instruments of novelty for one another.[28] Every human life, therefore, is a co-production: it needs the possibilities given by God, and it needs its own subjective agency to receive the lure of God and implement it. Identity will emerge from both God's contribution to each occasion and to some measure of self-creation.

As mentioned earlier, Charles Harthsorne reflected on Whitehead's dipolar notion of God and suggested that God's perfection must be defined in a way that includes supreme sensitivity, sympathetic dependence, and the possibility of his self-surpassing experience of new value. He must enjoy our joy and grieve with our sorrows. He writes that "what one cannot do is to fail . . . to derive at least some value from the joys (of others) through the act of recognition itself, and precisely the most perfect mind would derive most from the satisfaction of others."[29] God, therefore, has an abstract and absolute character that is all knowing and all loving and immutable, i.e., his *absolute* character never changes and never becomes. But his abstract and absolute character is balanced by a *concrete*, relative side. In other words, the ways in which God's absolute character is actually expressed are constantly becoming, i.e., God's immediate experience is shaped by the character and destiny of what he knows. God is super-relational, and no one is more thoroughly shaped by experience than God. Both of these are then aspects of a concrete and dynamic reality who is related to the world by his love and compassion.[30]

This dipolar understanding of God for Hartshorne is not a difficult concept to grasp (again) if we consider first our own analogously dipolar structure. In fact, the dipolar understanding of humankind is the one that can be employed analogously to try to render meaningful or conceptually coherent the scriptural understanding of God. The dipolar concept for God is real but analogous, for in *both* "poles" of his reality God alone is *supremely* perfect. In his abstract "pole" God alone is absolute. For he alone among all realities is not dependent on others for his existence. In his concrete "pole," however, God, like us, is relative. But again here, Hartshorne introduces a qualitative difference: God alone is relative to *all* other beings. He alone affects and is affected by all others.

Even such crucial "historical" figures, i.e., those thinkers or actors who affect lives on a major scale, such as an Aquinas or a Marx were affected by and affect a still relatively small number of persons. On the contrary, as "the great companion — the fellow-sufferer who understands" in Whitehead's famous formulation,[31] God alone is relative to all.

Therefore, in both versions of divine polarity, there is immutability and mutability. Both Whitehead and Hartshorne "have shifted the philosophical consideration of God away from the notions of his omnipotence as a creator who has control *over* a world which he necessarily transcends, to his ongoing creative relationship of love *with* a world in process."[32] Rather than exclude God from the world, they include the world in their notion of God. "God is completed by the individual, fluent satisfactions of finite fact . . . ," writes Whitehead.[33]

God alone affects all (by providing the relevant possibilities) and is affected by all (by himself changing as our actual decisions and actions occur and affect him). The dipolar-God alone is *both* absolute *and* supremely relative. This dipolar concept, then, is the only coherent way by which Whitehead and Hartshorne believe we can affirm the central scriptural insight that a loving and related God alone is God.

The panentheism which Charles Hartshorne proposes includes the world in a God who is more than world, and in that sense transcendent.[34] God's love has extended his selfhood to include all of creation. Hartshorne has a magnificent passage on God's involvement in human existence: "God orders the universe . . . by taking into his own life all the currents of feeling in existence. He is the most irresistible of influences precisely because he is himself the most open to influence. In the depths of their hearts all creatures (even those able to 'rebel' against him) defer to God because they sense him as the one who alone is adequately moved by what moves them. He alone not only knows but feels . . . how they feel, and he finds his own joy in sharing their lives, lived according to their own free decisions, not fully anticipated by any detailed plan of his own. Yet the extent to which they can be permitted to work out their own plan depends on the extent to which they can echo or imitate on their own level the divine sensitiveness to the needs and precious freedom of all . . . This is a vision of a deity who is not a supreme autocrat, but a universal agent of 'persuasion', whose 'power is the worship he inspires' . . ."[35] God is distinguished from the world but at the same time is interiorly modified and manifests himself in relation with the world. Karl Rahner and Herbert Vorgrimler maintain that God and the world are "the reciprocal conditioning of unity and difference as they grow in the same proportion . . . This doctrine of the 'immanence' of the world in God is false and heretical only if it denies creation and the distinction of the world from God (and not only of God from the world)."[36] What happens in the world affects God who in turn affects the world. God's love "passes into the world. The love in the world passes into God and floods back again into the world."[37] There is then a deep sense of the intimacy between God and history. It might be called a theory of inter-active relationality in which the world both receives effects from God and affects God.

The Catholic theologian David Tracy has noted the present unwillingness of the "transcendental tradition" in Catholic thought (as represented by Rahner and Lonergan) "to break with the classical theistic concepts of Aquinas." Tracy states his conviction that "classical Christian theism is neither internally coherent nor adequate as a full account of our common experience and of the scriptural understanding of the Christian God."[38] Here Tracy recommends the philosophy of Hartshorne to the critical attention of all Christian theologians. "To my knowledge," he writes, "no other single thinker in modernity has proposed as carefully formulated and evidential a series of alternatives to the classical dilemmas of theists and non-theists alike."[39]

If God can be known as real, it is because God is immanent in the world. We can move from the world to God, but never in the opposite direction. This has been classified as "doing theology from below" by Piet Schoonenberg.[40] There has been a tendency at times "to imagine that knowledge and understanding of life, especially when it concerns God, takes place in some rarified region of man's mind in isolation from his ordinary everyday experience. In fact, however, such knowledge and understanding of life and of God is always rooted in man's multiple experiences of the world around him."[41]

Since God is disclosed as immanent only within our experienced world, process theologians would find it very difficult to deal with theological formulations that speak of God as the "Totally Other." For them, our knowledge of God will always bear the same trademarks as our perception and understanding of the world. God is available *in* experience; ultimacy is given *in* the immediacy of lived experience. Perhaps Norman Pittenger expresses this most coherently when he writes: "Process thought is the name usually given to that view of the world which takes with utmost seriousness the dynamic living, evolutionary quality of our existence and of the world in which we live. Ours is not a world of unchanging substances, of fixed entities, or permanently located 'nows' and 'thens'; it is a world in change, in which we have to do *not* so much with *being* as with *becoming* and in which we find ourselves caught up in processive movements rather than imprisoned in fixed habitations. From its lowest components — societal energies at the subatomic level — up to the highest grades known to us, we see this same energizing dynamic quality. . . The *principle of explanation* of such a world must in some genuine fashion be *like* that world. . . God cannot, in such a world, be the exception to the metaphysical principles required to understand the world, but must be the *chief exemplification* of those principles. God is living, dynamic, energizing. He is also *related*. The perfection which can be claimed for him is not that proper to some unmoved or absolute essence; it is the perfection of his own identity as being himself, but that perfection subsists in his identity *in* and *with* relationships. He is the One who is sufficient to remain himself even while he *constantly surpasses himself* in his expression and activity. What happens in the world contributes to his satisfaction, enriches his possibilities in further self-expression, and provides ever new opportunities for his loving care."[42] Value is always the outcome of limitation.

* * * * *

We have seen then how process thought challenges and reinterprets the understanding of God of the classical Christian tradition. Process thinkers affirm with the tradition that the existence of God is the only possible final understanding of our human situation. But they deny that the *nature* of God as understood and expressed by that tradition is sound. They affirm that God is the supremely perfect one, but they deny that the concept of perfection excludes change and process in God himself. They affirm with the scriptural tradition that fundamentally God is Love, but insist that Christians can only *mean* this statement when they reject the concept of a changeless, non-relative being articulated by classical Christian theism. They deny that the most usual concept employed to communicate that tradition, namely, the understanding of God as self-subsistent being unaffected by our actions, is either coherent or scriptural.

For is not the God of the Jewish and Christian scriptures a God profoundly involved in humankind's struggle to the point where he not merely affects but is affected by the struggle? Is Bonhoeffer's famous cry that *"only a suffering God can help"* a merely rhetorical flourish of a troubled man? Can Christians *mean* the most fundamental religious affirmation of Christian self-understanding if they simultaneously affirm the usual understanding of classical Christianity that God is the self-subsistent, changeless, omniscient, all-powerful one who is not really (*relatio entis*) but only notionally (*relatio rationis*) affected by humankind's actions?

If God rules the world, it is by the power of love, not by maintaining complete control over the lives of his creatures and manipulating the environment around them. Belief in God as love is nothing new for Christians; it has always been singled out as the highest perfection for God and humankind. Process theology simply takes that premise and draws it to its logical conclusion. It shows that God cannot be so powerfully active and perfectly independent that he is unmoved by the love of his adopted children.

Love in the fullest sense involves a sympathetic response to the one loved. It means feeling with the feelings of another, hurting with the pain of another, grieving with the grief, rejoicing with the joys. That God is such a lover is evidenced by the incarnation wherein he assumed the condition of our humanity and joined us in our journey through life. If we who are "made in the image and likeness of God" are expected to be compassionate and sympathetic with one another, surely our creator must be just as *internally* involved with us.

Traditional theism defines God as completely impassive, the unmoved mover who cannot possibly be affected by what goes on outside him. God loves us only in the sense that he does good things for us, but not in the sense that he is with us in our feelings or responds to our love for him. Our love for God does nothing for him except contribute to his *external* glory. Internally, God is untouched by what transpires in the universe.

The reason for this lack of reciprocity is that God does not really relate to the world. The relationship is merely one of reason or idea, according to Thomas Aquinas. In the *Summa Theologiae* I, Q. 13, Art. 7, he writes: "Since, therefore, God is outside the whole order of creation, and all creatures are ordered to him, and not conversely, it is manifest that creatures are really related to God himself whereas in God there is no real relation to creatures, but a relation only in idea." God relates to the world as giver, but the relationship is a one-way street. Being pure act, God is incapable of receiving anything from the world. He simply goes about the business of doing his best for us, loving us in an outgoing way, as active good will, but in no sense responsive to or in need of our love.

For traditional theology, a truly responsive love on the part of God would be a sign of imperfection and weakness. It would indicate his need to wait on us before acting on our behalf. Process theology insists that all love is responsive and God as the supreme lover must be the most responsive of all, adapting and accommodating his goodness to our specific needs and desires.

Is not intelligent and responsible change a positive and not negative factor in all our experience? For example, does not John Henry Cardinal Newman's famous dictum "To live is to change and to be perfect is to have changed often" find resonance in our most fundamental outlook on our lives? The modern person does affirm change as a genuine perfection. For a consistent modern Christian, the process theologians argue, change (like all perfection) should be applied to God. Process is not only not an imperfection but it is the very condition for being real. An "event" is precisely what it means to be real. There is an implication here that every occasion of experience is partly determined and partly free. Freedom means that there are genuine options. Freedom is the ability to respond to those options (to a lesser or greater degree), and is therefore an exercise in process or self-creation. At lower levels, the "event" (the basic unit of reality) of freedom is experienced as some degree of behavioral spontaneity, as, e.g., in electron occasions. There is the principle of indeterminacy even in an electron "event." Consequently, the interplay between determination and freedom belongs to the process character of all reality.

For process theologians, to speak of divine omniscience is to say that at any given moment God knows everything that is knowable at that time. He knows the past inside out because it has already happened and he was there when it happened. He knows everything about the present because his grasp of what is is comprehensive and complete. As the wellspring for all that is yet possible, God knows what can and might happen in the future. What he cannot know in advance are the future free events yet to be decided by people. For those, he too must wait and see, like everyone else.

To know the actual future in advance would be tantamount to denying the reality of time as a series of events still in the process of being realized. It would be to imply that eternity already encompasses the whole of time and that nothing new happens under the sun that has not been previously worked out. Claiming that divine foreknowledge is compatible with human freedom because "knowing" is one thing and "determining" another does not work. In God, knowledge and power are one and the same. If it takes God time to work out his power in history, it seems equally reasonable to believe that his knowledge of history takes time as well.

Whether God forces the issue or not, any knowledge of the future can only be certain and unerring if the event is already fixed and determinate. So long as God wants us to be truly free, he is more than willing to be patient with us, both in the exercise of his power and in his coming to know the future.

We are told in the Gospel of Luke 2:52 that Jesus "grew in wisdom, age and grace". If we are to believe contemporary scripture scholars, this growth occurred not only with respect to the ordinary conditions of human living, but also with respect to the consciousness of his mission as messiah. If, as Son of God, Jesus knew everything, growth of this sort would be out of the question. The Son of God entered history not only to save it, but to learn about it as well. There is nothing like getting into the fray to know what it is all about! The incarnation was God's way of coming to know the meaning of time and history firsthand.

Walter Burghardt, S.J., has some illuminating observations about the Good Samaritan story in Luke 10:25-37, especially v. 33 "had compassion." He writes: "In biblical Greek this is a remarkable word . . . You know how you and I speak of the heart as the seat and source of our emotions, our feelings . . . Where we say 'heart,' they (the Jews) often said 'bowels.' They spoke especially of the bowels of love and affection, the bowels of mercy and sympathy and compassion. . . There is something still more remarkable about this biblical word for compassion. When it is used in the Gospels, it is used only of God the Father or of Jesus the Christ. In his famous song of praise, the father of John the Baptist extols the 'bowels of mercy of our God' (Lk. 1:78); the king (of heaven) forgives the servant in debt to him 'out of the bowels of his compassion' (Mt. 18:27); the father of the prodigal — really God the Father — runs to meet his repentant son because he is 'moved by the bowels of his compassion' (Lk. 15:20). Similarly for Jesus. This strong word strikes us when Jesus has compassion on crowds that are hungry (Mt. 15:32), and other crowds [cf. e.g., Mt. 14:14; Mt. 9:36; Mk. 1:41; Mt. 20:34; Mk. 9:22; Lk. 7:13].

Yes, this strong expression, 'bowels of compassion,' the Gospels use of God the Father and His only Son. There is but one exception: the Good Samaritan . . . Like God, like the God-man, the Samaritan 'sympathized' to the depths of his being . . . It may well be true that in the Father, as the Epistle of James declares, 'There is no variation of shadow due to change' (Jas. 1:17). But it is just as true that this changeless God loves us, has compassion for our woundedness, in the only way God can: I mean, with the whole of His being, the totality of His Godness. On this, Scripture is eloquent. Psalm 103 is but one example:

> The Lord is merciful and gracious,
>> Slow to anger and abounding in steadfast love . . .
> He does not deal with us according to our sins,
>> nor requite us according to our iniquities.
> For as the heavens are high above the earth,
>> so great is His steadfast love . . .
> As a father has compassion on his children,
>> so the Lord has compassion on those who fear him.
>> (Ps. 103: 8-13)

[cf. also Ezek. 33:11 and Isa. 49:15]. In Jesus God's compassion took flesh. You see, Jesus is not merely a wonderfully compassionate man, a soft touch for every brand of human misery. He is, in the pregnant and profound expression of Scripture, 'God with us.' God . . . with . . . us. In him God enters history as a suffering God, a God who wore our weakness, felt our fright, swallowed our bitter cup of rejection and loneliness. On this the Epistle to the Hebrews is eloquent (cf. Heb. 4:15-5:8). The compassion of Jesus is not a virtue he plucked now and again from a pigeonhole and applied to needy cases. He is compassion incarnate, God's compassion in weak human flesh. Everything he did, living or dying, welled up from the bowels of his compassion.''[43]

Perhaps even the opposite notion and emotion can be attributed to God. Without <u>humor</u> not even God can survive!

*   *   *   *   *

It would appear that at least three exciting consequences follow from the preceding observations:

1)   Spirituality must be deeply incarnational, attentive to the concreteness and vividness of lived experience as the bearer, discloser, and uncoverer of God; in brief, what is asked of us is a deep affection for the earth. This is a major shift in Christian asceticism. For example, many times in devotional or liturgical prayer we prayed to God to ''help us to keep our eyes lifted to heaven and to despise the things of the earth.'' The spirituality of Teilhard de Chardin is one example of an evolutionary process perspective that attempts to take the earth seriously as the bearer of God.

2)   The mystery and splendor of the human vocation is heightened greatly due to the fact that because of God's love for us and his receptivity, we can enrich or impoverish God's own life. God is the most ''event-ful'' of all that is.

3)   A reconciliation is now understandable between two strands of the Christian tradition: a *speculative* theology that endorsed an immutable God and an *ascetical* theology addressed to a mutable God, who can be moved and persuaded by what we do. It might very well be that Christians have always intuited a dipolar God. We, therefore, lived as spiritual schizophrenics because we believed in both ''poles'' but found ourselves incapable of putting them together. We worked with an inherited Greek worldview which maintained that to be perfect meant incapability of change. This meant, of course, that there could be no ''becoming'' in the experience of God; that God could have no real relationship with the world because such a relationship would imply change. Yet, our behaviors and our piety have certainly believed that what we do makes a real difference in God. For example, when the Christian would pray, ''O, my God, I am heartily sorry for having offended you,'' our instincts really felt that our sinfulness was painful to God.

John Shea offers a powerful summarization of the meaning of process theology when he comments that ''God's relationship to the world is viewed as the preeminent member of a community to the entire community. Between God and the world there is mutuality and interdependency. God acts in the world only in cooperation with other entities. Neither God nor the world act independently. The unit of activity is God-World. God is the ground of both order and novelty. He not only structures the possible forms of relationships but presents novel possibilities to those relationships. God has an initial aim for every moment of experience. Human freedom responds to and actualizes that aim to the extent that it is willing and able. God then becomes the lure, the evocation toward the increase of value. God is not a monarch but a fellow sufferer, not a tyrant but a loving parent who encourages but never forces. The human person is the co-creator of every moment.''[44]

If anything is immutable in God, it is the completeness of his love for humankind, which must include receptivity to our ever-changing needs and desires. Walter Brueggemann has commented that although '''covenant' is not the simple overarching theme of the Bible as previously claimed . . . nonetheless, it has important potential for the church in our situation. . . It subverts a theology that knows too much, a God who is too strong, a church that is too allied with triumphalistic culture, and a ministry that moves too much from strength. . . The covenanting God of the Bible makes a break with all cultural definitions and expectations. . . The primal disclosure of the Bible is that this God in heaven makes a move toward earth to identify a faithful covenant partner, responding to the groans of oppressed people (Exod. 2:24-25). . . This move is decisive not only for earth, but for heaven; not only for the slaves embraced, but for the God who embraces. It is central to covenant that this One cannot embrace without being transformed by the ones who are embraced. There is no immunity for God here; embracing a partner is not an after-thought, but is definitional for God. . . The break that God makes is to leave the self-sufficient world of the gods for the sake of groaning humanity. . . This God has made a break with the boredom of the canopy of heaven. . . God in heaven has committed all his godhood to the wayward partner. God has no other claim to make, no special exemptions for himself, but stays with the sorry partner; in the process, both are changed. . . To test its subversive impact, one need only teach it and preach it. For it represents a break with conventional theology. It calls into question the self-sufficiency of God, the entire catechetical tradition of a God without solidarity with earthly partners whom he values and makes valuable. The conventional God of the catechism makes all his caring moves *after* everything is settled and there is nothing at stake for the Strong One. But here it is affirmed that not everything is settled in advance. Very much is at stake for God; for godhood is re-characterized and re-decided in company with and in the presence of the mixed multitude. . . Covenant requires a radical break not only with uncritical, scholastic notions of God, but also with contemporary views that vote for detachment. Our current consumer culture has need of an irrelevant God for whom nothing is at issue, a kind of indifferent, immune guarantor. Such a God is challenged and destroyed in the claim of covenant. The alternative God of the Bible is impinged upon and exposed. . . The one for whose image we have settled is a sure, triumphant God who runs no risks, makes no commitments, embraces no pain that is definitional. . . That, perhaps, is the most important and most subversive thing the *church* can now do: to refuse to give up on the world and its promised transformation. . . These affirmations are a fragile minority report when they come to embodiment in Jesus of Nazareth who had so little power.''[45]

There is a massive humility that appears in the theistic metaphysics of Whitehead and Hartshorne. For although they maintain that God is infallibly present in the world, we must maintain an awareness that all the forms, and symbols, and theological reflections that mediate our religious experience are fallible. In the year 2001 C.E. theologians might read some process thinkers, and say: "Those process theologians! Were they ever dumb!" Our present forms and symbols that mediate God are perspectival, limited, conditioned, and never to be absolutized. God is always "beyond God" (to paraphrase Tillich), the iconoclast *par excellence* who over and over breaks out of the formulations and symbolizations that we make in our attempt to explore him in his mysterious presence. There is a saying in Zen Buddhism that "if you are going to point out the moon to some people, don't point with your finger too long, for some will begin to mistake your finger for the moon."

If process thinkers need any words of consolation, they might recall the remarks of Rollo May who says that "those we call saints rebelled against an outmoded and inadequate form of God on the basis of their new insights into divinity. The teachings that led to their deaths raised the ethical and spiritual levels of their societies. They were aware that Zeus, the jealous god of Mount Olympus, would no longer do. Hence, Prometheus stands for a religion of compassion. They rebelled against Yahweh, the primitive tribal god of the Hebrews who gloried in the deaths of thousands of Philistines. In place of him came the new visions of Amos and Isaiah and Jeremiah of the god of love and justice. Their rebellion was motivated by new insights into the meaning of godliness. They rebelled, as Paul Tillich has so beautifully stated, against God in the name of the God beyond God. The continuous emergence of the God beyond God is the mark of creative courage in the religious sphere."[46]

III. CONSEQUENCES FOR CHRISTOLOGICAL RE-APPROPRIATION

In the general context of process theology, the thought of W. Norman Pittenger and John B. Cobb, Jr. will now be examined with special emphasis on their Christological insights. Since Pittenger and Cobb are greatly indebted to Charles Hartshorne's critique of classical theism and his development of his own version of theism in which God is both concrete and abstract, absolute and relative, it might be proper to assess the relevance of his concepts to the area of Christology. The difficulty with this procedure is that it is an attempt to deal systematically with an aspect of Hartshorne's thought which is peripheral to his principal thematic emphasis. Nevertheless, such an approach seems demanded by the nature of David Tracy's invitation in *Blessed Rage for Order.*

For Hartshorne, classical theism is "a mere abstraction from the contingent and caused actuality of the divine life."[47] Being is an abstraction from becoming. God must be both being and becoming, being in his abstract aspect, becoming in his concrete actuality. This means that God's present concrete actuality is contingent. That God exist is necessary; but this necessity is an abstraction from God's concrete actuality. The abstract necessity of God's existence is the fundamental metaphysical principle.[48]

Hartshorne's God must be able to truly interact with his creatures. His knowing us as contingent cannot leave him unaffected *internally.* For "God in his concrete actuality being the inclusive whole requires all things."[49] The God of Hartshorne is a suffering God. He feels with us and understands. "Neo-classical theism can say and mean, 'God is love'."[50] In fact, Hartshorne even comments that "God is a spectator of all existence, but a sympathetic spectator who in some real sense shares in the sufferings he beholds. He is neither simply neutral to these sufferings nor does he sadistically will them for beings outside himself. He takes them into his own life and derives whatever value possible from them, but without ever wanting them to occur."[51]

As we shall see, it would appear that Hartshorne does not see the historical event of the Incarnation, a contingency that acts as the reconciliation of the divine and the human, as *necessary* in any strict sense. For him, a world is required, but it does not have to be any particular world. Therefore, there would be little room for any fall or redemption based on finite human decisions, a redemption in which the historical contingency of Jesus would have decisive finality. Hartshorne seems to contend that the finality of Jesus is a Hellenistic idea. But that can be argued only at the expense of the apocalyptic context of Jesus' life and preaching.

This brief summarization of Hartshorne's main conclusions has been intended to serve as a preliminary to one of the peripheral aspects of his thought — Christology. He suggests that this new dipolar view of God is "in some respects at least, a return to the gospel conception."[52]. There is an intuition which Hartshorne considers central to the religious perception of God, but which has been lost in classical theology, largely through the influence of Greek philosophy. He argues that an examination of religious practice in the "high religions" will reveal "divine human reciprocity as essential to religion."[53] Without this interaction between creature and creator, all the basic analogies such as "Father," "Ruler," "Friend," etc., collapse. In the interpretation of Hartshorne, the logic of classical theism (which takes God to be *the* absolute) prevents the conception of this interaction which is essential to religious practice. This contradiction is especially evident in Anselm's absolutist conception of deity.[54] He laments the fact that the claims of theistic religion have become historically tied to a given philosophy, e.g., Neo-Platonic or Aristotelian philosophy.[55] He even argues that the supposed harmony between Greek philosophy and the Bible is an illusion.[56]

Hartshorne has a predilection for the "tradition which comes down from Israel." He even writes that "no doubt there are strands in the Christian tradition which are unhelpful from the point of view I have been expounding. . . Yet whatever difficulties one has with the tradition which comes down from Israel, the correctives for those difficulties seem always to be available in that tradition if one looks for them."[57] He also adds in another article a personal confession that reads as follows: "I discern some degree of rational justification for a religion of complete all-inclusive devotion to One in whose life all good and all actuality are embraced, to whom prayer may properly be addressed, and whose loving acceptance even of our sufferings is supremely symbolized in the human life depicted in the gospels.''[58]

The affirmation that "Jesus Christ is Lord" can be considered the most central proclamation of Christian faith. It has been traditionally understood to imply the divinity of Jesus and the notion of God's incarnation in him. We must now ask then: what happens to this central Christian affirmation and the traditional understanding of it in the context of Hartshorne's philosophy? Hartshorne has stated that he has no Christology to offer and that he doesn't wish to criticize anyone else's.[59] Given the clear Christological implications of his concept of God, however, it seems difficult to interpret this posture as anything more than rhetorical.[60]

Hartshorne's concept of God sets a limit upon the logical possibilities open to Christology. For example, some process theologians have distinguished two types of Christology: historical or confessional Christology and constitutional or abstract Christology.[61] In Hartshorne's concept of God (as in Whitehead's) the notion of incarnation itself already has a central role to play. Hence any possible understanding of God's incarnation in Christ must be worked out in relationship to the larger notion of incarnation. Hartshorne suggests that among the analogies which have been used by religious language to convey God's personal character, the mind-body analogy is "indispensable."[62]

Simply stated, in this analogy the relationship between God and the world, with "world" as including all levels of life, is likened to the relationship between mind and body, such that God becomes, in a sense, the "soul" of the cosmos, and we become, in a sense, part of God's "body." We are actual parts of Hartshorne's God. This helps to explain how we can't help but intuit God.[63] This might very well explain why the theological commentator Colin Gunton has written the following critique: "From a theological point of view it can be said that because in process theology the world takes the place of the Son as that which is essentially related to the Father, man comes to know God directly without the mediation of Jesus Christ."[64] It might also be remembered that Whitehead had stated that "the world lives by its incarnation of God in itself."[65]

If the world is, in some sense, God's "body," then this is the *primary* mode of incarnation. Therefore to speak of God as incarnate in Jesus or of Jesus' divinity is to speak symbolically or metaphorically with reference to the prime instance of incarnation. This metaphor became necessary in the tradition because of the inability of the classical theist (due to the philosophical as opposed to the religious strand in historical theology) to speak of God literally, e.g., as literally suffering.[66]

Therefore, Hartshorne proposes that certain religious truths were "wrapped up" (so to speak) in the erroneous historical theory of a divine incarnation in Jesus. What then, he asks, was symbolized by the doctrine that the man on the cross was deity? To say that Jesus was God is another way of saying that God shares our suffering. The cross also tells us symbolically why the world is tragic. It is another way of saying that the root cause of suffering and tragedy lies in limited human freedom and the inevitable conflicts that arise because there is a plurality of free finite subjects. Also, the cross teaches us that there is an inner conflict within free individuals themselves.[67]

Considering the church as the "mystical body" of the life of Christ in history gave classical theists a way "to relate our lives in time to the divine life."[68]

For Hartshorne, contemporary philosophy provides a way to make *literal* and direct affirmations about God which, due to the logic of classical absolutist theism, had to be made indirectly, i.e., they had to be made as affirmations about God in Christ. The affirmation of the divinity of Jesus is therefore no longer necessary, nor is it internally consistent.[69]

It might be pertinent here to add the following observations lest the above citations from Hartshorne appear too shocking. Has there ever been or can there ever be a form of theism which will enable such phrases as "Jesus was God" or the "divinity of Jesus" to have a sufficiently unambiguous meaning that they would be entitled to serve as requirements for Christian unity? The most they can do is to name a mystery which is felt rather than thought; and people may well feel differently about different ways of phrasing the mystery. There is a double ambiguity here. On the one hand, no one can be human and *in every sense* also God. This would not be mystery, but simple contradiction. To be God is, e.g., to know all things; to be human is to know in limited fashion (as more or less bounded by the senses and discursive inference). To assert *both unqualifiedly* of the same subject is merely to talk nonsense. On the other hand, if it is only *in some sense* that Jesus was God, then we must remember that in some sense or some degree every person is God. He/she is an expression (Logos) of the divine life, as are all things whatever (even though not all are in accord with the divine ideal aim for them). Therefore, it seems probable that any doctrine of the divinity of Jesus must do one of the following:

1) assert and deny the same predicates of one logical subject;
2) assert the truism that a certain man (like all things, but more richly or purely than others) is a manifestation of divine love; or
3) leave it indeterminate, uncertain, or vague as to what (between these useless extremes) is asserted.

Possibly one could define a sufficiently *distinctive* sense in which, without contradiction, Jesus could be both God and human; but, unless and until this can be done, to make acceptance of the phrases in question a test of being a Christian is unwittingly to make a low degree of intellectual penetration — or honesty — an important factor in religious correctness. And this cannot be realistically desired!

Hartshorne proposes that historical Christianity (ecumenically considered), in addition to the choices of continuing in orthodoxy or rejecting the doctrines of the incarnation and the trinity, has a third possible alternative. He remarks that "it may extract from these doctrines the conceptions of man and God which they seem to have had the function to express, under the limitations of ancient philosophy and literalistic Biblicism."[70] In Hartshorne's philosophy, the traditional affirmation that Jesus Christ is Lord comes to mean that the man Jesus experienced the central religious insight that God is love more vividly than any other person, and that in his life, and especially in his death, this love is supremely and uniquely symbolized. As we shall see, John Cobb, in his book *Christ in a Pluralistic Age*, has developed these process affirmations into a compelling Christology which attempts to be faithful both to critical reason and Christian faith.

To summarize: both Whitehead and Hartshorne maintain that the world lives by the incarnation of God in itself. That is true of every "drop of experience." Jesus Christ, therefore, is not the only incarnation of God in history. However, it is the faith of the Christian that Jesus the Christ does something really spectacular in that particular incarnational event. This sometimes will sound abrasive to our inherited traditions and instincts. Yet, it is important to remember that the Jesus-Event is finite; it happens in history; it is historically and culturally conditioned. By that very fact it cannot be a definitive or exhaustive disclosure of who the mystery of God is. There is no historical event (person) that can "grab" everything there is to "grab" of the mystery of God and make it available in one disclosure. Remembrance of that will make Christians more tolerant of those disclosures of God that occur all over the world — and of what God might be saying through a Hindu or Buddhist or Moslem tradition.

In so far as the New Testament context for the affirmation that Jesus is the Christ and Lord lies in biblical eschatology, specifically in Jesus' particular version of late Jewish apocalyptic, "Christ" can only have a limited meaning in Hartshorne's philosophy. Like Neo-Platonic "logos" speculation, Hartshorne's philosophy is really cosmology. His Christology takes its point of departure in his concept of God — and it seems to exhibit the same tendencies characteristic of cosmological "logos" speculation on Jesus, which began "from above" with the concept of incarnation.[71] Origen, it might be remembered, had a similar problem of explaining how the union of the "Logos" with the man Jesus is different from his union with other creatures, e.g., in mystical experience. As we shall see, John Cobb faces this difficulty head on since he grounds his speculative Christology in the Jesus of history. Cobb has obviously gone beyond Hartshorne in the direction of defining a sufficiently distinctive sense in which, without contradiction, Jesus could have been both God and human. But whether this is possible within the speculative strictures of Hartshorne's philosophy, or further, whether it successfully overcomes the subordinationist tendencies associated with "Logos Christology," are further questions.

In spite of Hartshorne's assertions of the affinity of his categories to biblical speech, his *cosmological* conception does seem to tend in the opposite direction from the *historical* framework of biblical eschatology. In the latter framework, God separates himself from the world and is thereby capable of intervening decisively in its history. Even the biblical creation story is to be interpreted according to the maxim that eschatology precedes protology. But perhaps the types "cosmos" and "history" can be opposed in such a way as to say that Hartshorne's world is a "cosmos" and the biblical world is a "history."

There is genuine novelty in Hartshorne's cosmos, even though these do not affect the outcome of the process which has no beginning and no end. Rather, the novelties are absorbed into the life of God. Value can be maximized, but regardless of whether it is or not, the process will go on. Hartshorne's philosophy requires that there be novelty. However, it does not require that any *particular* novelty, e.g., the Exodus or Jesus' preaching of the Kingdom, have the decisive significance for the outcome of history which the Jewish and Christian scriptures attribute to them. Although the scriptures are saturated with language about the images of redemption, it is difficult to conceive how this term could have even a metaphorical meaning with reference to Hartshorne's cosmos. Perhaps a distinction could be made between process and history: the former term would include the latter in the sense that the history of this planet is included in the larger whole of the universe. History thus understood could conceivably begin and end. Process could not.

Hartshorne's rejection of the traditional affirmation that Jesus is divine is based on some speculative historical assumptions. The first of these assumptions would be Hartshorne's apparent belief that the affirmation of the divinity of Jesus is based chiefly on the influence of Greek philosophy. This assumption might ignore the universalist tendency of Jewish eschatology, the logic of which may well have led the early Christians to venture into the ways of Greek philosophy in the first place. The second assumption follows naturally: the possible historical continuity between early Christian eschatology and the use of "logos" speculation by the Fathers. If this continuity is ignored, the New Testament traditions which implicity, at least, affirm the divinity of Christ have to be rejected as mythological. Hartshorne's philosophical speculation could lead the careless Christian exegete vis-à-vis "demythologization" to a position to the right of Bultmann.

From a critical point of view, the possibility must be admitted that a future scholarly consensus may well arrive at results that are quite compatible with the speculative demands of Hartshorne's *constitutional* Christology. For example, the issues of the centrality of apocalyptic in the preaching of Jesus and its present significance, the historicity of the resurrection, etc., may take on totally different contours in possible future critical developments. However, given the present pluralist situation and given the weight of tradition for such affirmations as the divinity of Christ or the historicity of the resurrection, it would seem illogical to dismiss these affirmations on purely speculative grounds. Hartshorne's system, when applied to Christology, might easily be labeled a de-eschatologized theism.

Ralph James has attempted to sketch the outline of an *ecclesiology* consciously constructed on Hartshorne's philosophy.[72] Such a church would rest on the foundation of Hartshorne's affirmations about Jesus: the experience of God was more present to him than to any other person, and his life (especially his death) supremely symbolizes the religious insight of God as suffering love. Therefore, the church would be the concrete response to the actual occasion of Jesus, the fellowship of all those responding to him. The Christian church would be "that series of occurrences taking Jesus Christ as their point of reference."[73]

The conceptual apparatus of Hartshorne's philosophy allows this fellowship to be conceived ecumenically. The priority of becoming over being, of the concrete over the abstract, disallows the dogmatic certainties upon which the historical divisions of Christianity are based by revealing the idolatrous nature of the dogmas themselves. The future of all institutions is contingent. Since there is no prescribed form in which historical Christianity has been foreordained to result, the churches of the present are free to create their own ecumenical future in as pluriform or unitary a mode as they see fit.[74]

This conception of an ecumenical Christian fellowship, freed from authoritarian dogmatism, is an attractive one. For Hartshorne, however, Christ is a purely contingent symbol. Therefore, a church founded "with reference" to him is likewise a purely contingent symbol for God's love. As a more or less *aesthetically* apt symbol, which is in a true sense an efficacious symbol, this church could not claim a revelation. It could not consider itself necessary in any respect.

What would motivate a person to join such a church? Simply the power of the symbol of Jesus, an aesthetic attraction to the symbol of Jesus. If the Christian specificity of such a church would simply be "reference to Jesus," then its visibility would most likely be such that one would not juridically join it, but simply be a metaphysical part of it. What James describes here may well become Christianity's future ecumenical form. A quick glance back at the history of Christianity in all its variety reveals that this possibility might not be as fantastic as it presently sounds.

Consequently, in the area of Christology, Christians are asked to look upon the divinity of Christ as a veiled affirmation, now no longer necessary, of God's suffering love. In Hartshorne's philosophy, the significance of Jesus is not to be understood in terms of biblical eschatology, but as a unique instance of God's *general* incarnation, no more unique perhaps than any other such instance. The finality of Jesus and any sense of his having accomplished an efficacious redemptive work is difficult to conceive of in Hartshorne's cosmos, where particularity as such is demanded, but no particular particularity can have final significance. Christian theologians already committed to a thorough-going "de-eschatologizing" on other grounds would find an intelligent alternative in Hartshorne.

However, it may be that "within the widened perspective of process thought on the meaning of the incarnation, Christians should admit a diversity of special mediators of God's self-revelation. It may be that a future chapter of theology will be devoted to a new polytheism, in the sense of a plurality of mediators whose relationship to Christ will be more equal and ecumenical than was hitherto thought possible.''[75]

* * * * *

W. Norman Pittenger believes that process thought provides a basis for a Christological statement which can make sense to modern persons and be adequate to the central intention of the traditional creedal affirmations. The task is to express the decisiveness of Jesus in relation to God while still affirming his full, historically conditioned manhood. This latter requirement entails that Jesus be conceived as *different in degree*, rather than *in kind*, from other men. The traditional discussion about the divinity of Jesus is interpreted as an "act of God" in him and is related explicitly to Whitehead's process conceptuality. Pittenger's central purpose is to show that, within Whitehead's conceptuality, Jesus can be thought of as fully human, as not different in kind from other humans, and yet can be ascribed a "speciality" which does justice to the intention of the traditional affirmations about him.[76]

There is a certain vagueness in Pittenger in regard to our historical knowledge of Jesus. He merely asserts that we can be certain that Jesus was essentially like "the overall impression conveyed by the Gospels . . . we have, at the very least, a highly probable portrait of a real man. . . There was precisely a 'that' in a historical figure which is continuous with the 'that' which Christian faith wishes to assert.''[77] Pittenger seems to lack a methodological discussion of the relationship between what most would distinguish as *historical* assertions about Jesus and *faith* assertions about his relationship to God. However, he in no way attempts to mitigate Jesus' historical conditionedness.

Pittenger sees God's incarnation in Jesus as "located" not solely in the discrete individual Jesus, but in the total event of which Jesus is the focusing center. Besides Jesus himself, the total event which can be appropriately designated by his name includes not only the long Jewish preparation for him but also the total response to him down to this very day. He also maintains that when Christians speak of the finality or decisiveness of Jesus, they should intend this not of Jesus apart from his consequences, but of "the complex reality of Christ in his Church."[78] Consequently, we can never talk about Jesus as separate from the Church, or about the Church as separate from Jesus. To grasp the significance of any person, past and present and future must be taken into account. God's activity in Christ cannot be discussed apart from the response to that activity (unless we want to talk in abstractions). A revelation by definition involves an accepting response to the event of Jesus the Christ.

It might be objected at this point that Pittenger has distorted and inconsistently used the Whiteheadian conceptuality of "prehensions." For Whitehead, prehensions apply to past occasions; the future is included in the present only as an aim or a hope. Future occasions are not prehended. But Pittinger seems to see future occasions also as prehended. For example, he intends the term "focusing" to be a synonym for Whitehead's "prehending" and therefore he can say that "every person . . . is to be seen as the focusing of the past, his present relationships, and the results of his appearance at some given time and place."[79]

In other words, Pittenger does not maintain Whitehead's position on internal and external relations, i.e., that an entity has internal relations to its past, but only external relations to those actualities which will be in its future. Pittenger seems to generally treat relations to the past and to the future as symmetrical. Therefore, he seems to see the way an actual entity will be prehended as essential to what it now is!

He believes this line of thought is supported by Whitehead's insistence that all the basic constituents of the world process are occasions of experience, so that objective and subjective, event and response, belong together. Hence, he feels that the Church is part of "the concrete actuality of the event of Christ."[80] In fairness to Pittenger it should be noted that he is not speaking of the ecclesiastical institution in its narrower sense. He is speaking of the "Church" as "the total effective result of Christ's coming as this impinged upon, changed, and gave meaning to the succeeding ages in history up to the present hour . . . some institutional form is not only inevitable, man being what he is, but is also required if the response is to make any quite concrete impact; the sad thing has been the freezing of that institutional form, so that for many it has become a strait-jacket rather than a liberating agency, while for others it has become an idolatrous substitute for the dynamic and vitalizing response in its proper fullness."[81]

Pittenger could be accused of avoiding the real task of Christology proper and of neglecting one of the chief advantages of Whitehead's thought for Christological reflection. The basic question of Christology is precisely whether the Christian response to Jesus has been appropriate to what Jesus himself was. The task of Christology proper is to present an interpretation which is credible (both historically and philosophically) of Jesus' person, meaning precisely that past reality that was Jesus of Nazareth, and which provides a justification for the decisive role he has in fact had in people's lives. The real question is whether the Christian estimation of Jesus' importance for humankind's relationship to God is based on a correct interpretation of Jesus' own relationship to God.

Within the conceptuality of Whitehead, it is not a falsifying abstraction to discuss Jesus in himself, apart from his consequences, e.g., the Church. In other words, we may never be able to talk about "the Church as separate from Jesus" but we can accurately talk about "Jesus as separate from the Church." In a Whiteheadian framework, occasions of experience are discrete realities, and are related to future consequences only *externally*, not constitutively. This could very well be one of the great merits of Whitehead's conceptuality for Christology: one can intend to talk about actualities as they were "in themselves," prior to their reception by others.

It would appear that in Pittenger's Christology the issues of person and significance are confused. For example, he can write: "What a man is, what he counts for, what he means . . . can be known only when we see him in association with others, influencing others and being influenced by them."[82] It is true that what a person is can only be known through his/her outer actions and reactions (i.e., relationality); but this statement of Pittenger also apparently equates what a person is with his/her significance. The future of any person is essential to his/her significance; but not to his/her identity or selfhood.

Further, Pittenger says that God's activity in Christ cannot be discussed apart from the response to that activity without talking in abstractions.[83] But this is the type of argument into which theologians who cannot talk about events in themselves and/or about God's causality are forced. Whitehead's realistic philosophy — and an adequate Christology — allows for talk of God's activity in human events apart from any response by subsequent events, accepting or otherwise. It is certainly true that an act of God would not have been a *revelation* apart from an accepting response; but if God did indeed act supremely in a certain event, then this event would have been the supreme *act* of God even if no one had prehended it as such. Because of this, Pittenger "makes no clear advance on the christologies of men such as Tillich and Bultmann, who for the most part reduce Christology to soteriology."[84]

The decisiveness of Jesus is interpreted by Pittenger primarily in terms of the "importance" which this event has had for us. He also maintains that Jesus Christ is what he does, and that therefore we should speak of "activities" operative in him rather than of his "natures."[85] This could well be a starting point for a proper process Christology, except that Pittenger in the same context identifies the "activities" of Jesus with his "benefits" (a concept he borrows from Melancthon). Consequently, to maintain that Jesus Christ is what he "does" leaves the verb "does" quite ambiguous. It can now be interpreted as not referring to Jesus' acting itself but to the *effects* of that action. Hence the meaning of the statement could easily be that Jesus Christ is the significance ("benefits") he has for others.

If this line of thought were followed consistently, there could be no normative statement (which would have its truth-value independently of people's actual response to Jesus) as to what kind of response is appropriate in light of the way that God was specially present or active in Jesus. Christology would then consist mainly of *descriptive* statements as to how Jesus has in fact been received; and *prescriptive* statements as to how Jesus should be received would remain arbitrary preferences.

Pittenger also defines the human Jesus as "the center and focus" of the total Christ-event;[86] as a "unity" in whom God and man are brought together in singular intensity;[87] and as a "point" at which God is acting in a manner unparalleled elsewhere.[88] The speciality of Jesus though must be discussed in terms of God's initial aims for people. God acts in human affairs in the same way that he acts everywhere, and God acts in Jesus in the same way that he acts in human affairs generally, i.e., by luring each being towards the fullest actualization of its potentialities.[89] The speciality of Jesus would therefore consist in the *almost immeasurable difference of degree* to which he actualized God's aim or vocational lure for him and hence his manhood.[90]

In these citations, Pittenger does talk directly about the person of Jesus and does try adequately to account for Jesus' speciality. Of course, he must do this, for even though he defines the event of Jesus Christ as including Jesus' total impact on history, he constantly refers to Jesus himself as the norm in terms of which the faithfulness of the Church is to be measured.[91] But in developing this line of thought he does seem to fail to use fully the possibilities provided by Whitehead's philosophy, i.e., the notion of God's "initial aim." He does not consistently maintain the distinction between "actual entities" and "enduring objects." More often than not, Pittenger speaks as if this term referred to God's aims for enduring objects. His language is unclear at times, but certainly the manner in which he relates "initial aim" to "enduring objects" gives the former concept much less specificity than it has in Whitehead. This is why he speaks *generally* of *an* initial aim (or "vocational lure") for an *entire* human life.[92]

Consequently, it would seem that Pittenger thinks that God has the same general aim for all people. He claims that God's "Logos" provides "the divinely given pattern for fulfillment."[93] Therefore, the initial aim given to different people would be identical, that aim being "completely realized manhood with the brethren and in God."[94] Pittenger can say that Jesus is the one in whom God actualized "in a living human personality the potential God-man relationship which is the divinely-intended truth about every man";[95] and that in Jesus "that which is a possibility" and "which in each of us is to some extent partially realized" is made real and factual.[96] Jesus is the fully adequate expression, the classic instance, of God's intention for humankind.[97]

This very generalized use of the notion of "initial aim" leads to a portrayal of Jesus as *different merely in degree* from other persons in their relation to God, a portrayal (it would seem) which fails to provide the sort of discontinuity which the Christian faith implies. The thought of Whitehead, on the other hand, might permit a type of difference which is more in harmony with the traditional Christian intention — as manifested in its dual rejection of Adoptionism and Pelagianism. Whitehead speaks clearly both of God's most general subjective aim and his particular aims for specific occasions. It would seem a legitimate extension of Whitehead to speak of various levels of divine purpose in between these two extremes. For example, one could speak of a general aim for rational creatures; this, of course, would have to be stated in highly formal terms. One could also speak of a slightly less general aim for rational creatures in a particular culture; and then of an even less general aim for an individual life. Furthermore, one could speak of an even more specific purpose for a certain period of a person's life before finally reaching the most specific level of purpose which refers to individual occasions.

The essential point here is that there are various levels at which the *content* of the divine purpose for people can be discussed, and that at the more specific levels there will be ever greater differences in content. For the divine aim is always for the actualization of that possibility which is best, given the total relevant context.[98]

Consequently, if one is discussing God's *general* aim for rational creatures, there will be no differences between God's aim for Jesus and his aim for all other people. If it makes sense to speak of a general aim for people in the Jewish culture at the time of Jesus, at this level there would be no difference between God's aim for him and for his Jewish contemporaries; but there would be differences in relation to his contemporaries in other cultures, for the backgrounds and relevant possibilities of these people would be quite different.

Finally, if one is speaking about God's aim for Jesus himself — particularly for specific occasions of Jesus' experience — the differences between the *content* of these divine aims and the aims for other people, and especially for those at different times and places, must be conceived to be very great indeed.

It would seem, however, that Pittenger speaks only of God's *generalized* aim or pattern for human fulfillment; it is apparently this which is the initial aim provided for each life and which Jesus fully actualized. In other words, he does not use the notion of more *specific* divine aims; and hence the correlative idea of the speciality in the *content* of the aims proferred to Jesus. It could be suggested that the content of those aims was special in the sense that their actualization would result in an optimal expression of God's eternal subjective aim and his subjective form of response to all finite actualities as well.

If Pittenger had used Whitehead's thought in this way, the speciality of Jesus would arise not simply by his actualizing to a much greater degree possibilities which are open to all people. Rather, Jesus' revelatory decisiveness would be rooted in the special content of God's agency in relation to him, as well as in Jesus' extraordinary response. Only the two together would account for God's special presence in Jesus.

Pittenger is concerned to avoid the arrogance involved in too exclusive claims for Christ.[99] It could be that the revisions suggested here would avoid that arrogance implied in the view that Jesus provides the material norm for humankind as such. One can rightly say that, *formally* speaking, Jesus provides a norm for humankind if in fact he optimally actualized God's special aims for himself, since the general or formal ideal for all people is that they actualize their own highest possibilities, i.e., the specific divine aims for them in each moment. But it is something else to point to Jesus as a *material* norm and suggest that only he is fully human! For, given the radically different ideal aims that must obtain for different people at different times and places, there is nothing inconsistent in supposing that other people have also actualized the divine aims for them to a very high degree, so that they too were fully human — without their also being especially good expressions or reflections of God's own subjective aim.

As mentioned earlier, the difference between people in relation to God need not be conceived merely in terms of degree of actualization or intensity (as Pittenger suggests[100]), but can also be thought to involve tremendous differences in *content* of divine aims and hence of presence. In another line of thought, the explanation for the decisiveness of Jesus by Pittenger does not seem to clearly distinguish act and response — and his appeal is apparently made primarily to the subjective response of Jesus. Since the idea of "incarnation" is central, Pittenger might have given an explanation as to the sense in which one entity can be said to be "present in" another. A discussion of the difference between *subjective immediacy* and *objective presence* would help avoid any suspicion that Pittenger's insistence upon the full humanity of Jesus is vitiated by his affirmation of God's presence to him and in him.

Pittenger therefore cannot seem to make any type of qualitative difference between Jesus and other people, but only a difference of degree. Also, when Pittenger develops the idea of Jesus' revelatory significance, it is the divine agency (manner of operation as persuasion) that is stressed, rather than also the divine nature, or character and purpose. This may be connected with his "ambivalence in regard to speaking about actualities in themselves and his preference for speaking of their activities."[101]

In summary, we might say with Richard McBrien that "Pittenger . . . concludes that Jesus is different from the rest of us in degree, not in kind. Jesus realized to an unsurpassable degree the possibilities open to us as human beings. Christ is divine only in the sense that the Love which is God is at work in and through him. If human beings have the capacity to live in love, it is Jesus Christ who fully actualizes that capacity. And so Christ and God are one with the other in Love."[102] [My comments here should not be taken as a harsh theological indictment of Pittenger. He is to be congratulated for his theological astuteness in taking Whiteheadian foundational thought to a vigorous and dynamic frontier of Christological exploration.]

*　*　*　*　*

John B. Cobb, Jr. has recently made a Whiteheadian Christological formulation one of his principal concerns. His Christological exploration is still in formation, and as late as 1975 his *Christ in A Pluralistic Age* was still acknowledged by him to be a "progress report." Cobb's Christology is his attempt to demonstrate how the claim of Jesus might be understood within the world-view and the philosophical categories of Whitehead. It is not a matter of substantiating or proving the claim. Cobb writes as a Christian, i.e., as one who is in some way already grasped by the claim. His purpose is to offer conceptuality in support of the claim. My comments here deal with Cobb's Christology prior to *Christ in a Pluralistic Age*.

The "claim" of Jesus that Cobb wishes to elucidate corresponds largely to the understanding of Jesus that has emerged from the theologians of the "new quest" of the historical Jesus, e.g., James M. Robinson.[103] Basically, Jesus claims a relation of extraordinary immediacy with God, intimate enough to experience God as "Abba", and to confer upon himself the authority to speak for God on his own: "he was a strange figure for any time and place. His teaching and action involved an implicit assumption or claim of authority that was *different in kind* rather than degree from the claim of other teachers of his time or of ours. The authority he implicitly claimed rested in himself rather than in received teachings or a fresh word from God. It was closely connected with a sense of relatedness to God such that he saw the response of men to his message and himself as decisive for their response to God or even identical with it."[104]

For Cobb, no understanding of Jesus can fail against the metaphysical categories. The one-world view of Whitehead makes that a requisite. That, by and large, is also a requirement of modern persons if religion is to get a hearing. But beyond that, if the life of Jesus is to make a full claim upon us, it must be a claim that offers a life of relationship to God and people into which we can enter.

Cobb first treats how God is present in Jesus, which of course must be in terms of the dynamics through which God is present at other points of creation. The essential meaning of "presence" is that of causal efficacy. In other words, "A" has something to do with "B's" becoming, and "A" is thereby present to "B". But there is a wide range of roles through which "A" is present to and in "B". The role of "A" in "B" is partly determined by "A" and partly by "B". For example, there is something about a friend that conditions how he/she is a friend to me, but there is also much about me that determines how I let my friend enter into my life and be present to me. Or in terms of past occasions to my experience, if "B" represents an almost total break with what I was just doing, e.g., a new decision, then what I was just doing — i.e., my "A" moment — plays a minimal role in my "B" moment. The presence of "A" is meager. But if "A" represents a decision that was just made, e.g., to listen very carefully to what someone is saying, then "B" (which is the succeeding moment) is very largely determined by "A". "A" has a large and highly effective presence.[195]

God is present to every act of becoming through the initial aim which makes possible the act of becoming. In each instance, the initial aim (what God offers) is absolutely unique; it is for this precise act of becoming to be its best self. That best self will reflect both the individual act of becoming in itself and in its relation to the rest of the world. The actual world out of which any concrescence's best self emerges is different from every other actual world, and therefore is unique as it taps the structure of possibility. The initial aim does not impose its configuration on the remaining phases of a concrescence. The concrescence is responsible for what it does with the initial aim. If what God offers (the initial aim) is kept more fully intact by the concrescence in its own subjectivity, the more fully God is present. Full fidelity to the call of God in the initial aim means no discrepancy between the call and the attainment. And there is a cumulative effect in this, i.e., cumulative fidelity to those successive aims offered by God means cumulative effectiveness of God's presence. The cumulative fidelity of Jesus to the call of God is one way that Cobb explains the extraordinary presence of God in and to Jesus. Such fidelity could only be achieved with extraordinary awareness and deliberate human choices, i.e., with consciousness of God's immediacy to one's act of becoming. And that is part of the claim of Jesus: the centrality and immediacy of God's presence to his very existence and his awareness of the fact.

Cobb also indicates that the presence of God to a person is not restricted to the prehensive objectification of God in the initial aim.

God can be prehended through a sense of his wider purposes and concern for the world. In the terminology of the New Testament, God can be present through a life which is spent in building up his Kingdom. A sense of what the Kingdom of God requires is a sensitivity through which God shapes what a person is. Concern for the Kingdom of God (the central motif of the preaching of Jesus) is a mode of God's presence. This centrality and strength of Jesus' concern for the Kingdom of God is still another way of dealing with the presence of God to history in and through Jesus.

The mode of God's presence to, in, and through Jesus is not an exception to the modes in which God is present to other entities. But the *call* issued through God's presence, in each subjective aim, is unique in every case. So it is in Jesus. And there is a certain facticity about each instance of God's call and the ramifications of that call. Jesus sensed a meaning for all people in the shape of his life. He sensed the immediacy of God's presence to him which he understood as unique, as giving him access to God that was nowhere else available, and therefore as giving others access to God through him. Why? When all is said and done there is something ultimate about a decision that is made that is not further reducible (which is what freedom means). And that ultimacy counts for the decisions of God expressed in the initial aim offered to each moment of process, and it counts equally for the decisions a person makes as he works out the configuration of his responsibility to and for the call of God.

James C. Carpenter comments that Cobb fashions "two distinct though related problems. First, there is the general problem of accounting for God's presence in any person without displacing some aspect of that person's humanity. Secondly, there is the special problem of accounting for God's unique presence in Jesus.[106] He works toward the resolution of these two problems through an amplification of the Whiteheadian notion that the presence within a presently concrescing actual occasion of a contiguously related occasion in its past does not necessarily conflict with the self-determination of the newly concrescing occasion."[107]

Cobb is careful to specify many times that both God and humankind are best characterized as living persons consisting respectively of societies of actual occasions.[108] It should be noted here that his view of God as a *living person* places him at some variance with Whitehead, since Whitehead prefers to treat God as an actual entity and nowhere refers to him as a living person. Cobb's reason for going beyond Whitehead in this regard is that he believes the treatment of God as a living person to be far more harmonious with Whitehead's own metaphysical assumptions throughout *Process and Reality*. He views Whitehead's failure to identify God as a living person as an oversight exposing a weakness in his own system which Cobb himself now proposes to correct.[109]

Cobb suggests that we should think of creatures as prehending God and of God as prehending creatures, and that "prehension" should have a univocal meaning here and when applied to the relation of creatures to other creatures. Neither Whitehead nor Cobb intend to give equality to God and individual creaturely occasions (persons). If something like equality, or at least polarity, is sought, it would be between God and the world as a whole. There is, for Cobb, inequality between God and human persons. His stress on the divine initiative seems to some theological commentators to deny or disparage the human freedom that is essential to every actual entity. Cobb simply says that in the way Whitehead understands divine initiative, it "operates always to optimize human freedom."[110]

The Whiteheadian view is that all human action expresses in some measure God's aim. Cobb admits that there are difficulties here both with respect to Whitehead's own teaching and with respect to its translation into theological language. However, Cobb understands that apart from God each occasion (if it could be at all) would be the *passive* resultant of the causal forces of the past. On the other hand, God opens to the occasion the possibility of creative novelty in its response to these forces. Human behavior that "would destroy the world, for example, might be the result either of unchecked causality of the past or free acts made possible by the divinely given transcendence over these forces. The latter would be an actualization of a possibility derived from God even if quite distinct from and opposed to God's ideal aim."[111]

Cobb's purpose very definitely is to provide a Whiteheadian Christology in which the distinctiveness of Jesus is *not* described in terms of *degrees* of obedience or conformity to the initial aim.

One of the extremely valuable contributions of John Cobb is his rather close substitution of "structure of existence" ("experience") for "nature." Every moment of process is a drop of experience, the experience of surveying the actual world and the world of possibility, and from that welter of material "getting it all together." The experience of "getting it together" constitutes the existence of an entity. An entity does not first exist and then take note of the world and of possibilities; it is the very act of incorporating other entities, or aspects of them, or new possibilities, that is constitutive of the entity's existence. The structure of an entity's "getting it together" is determinative of what an entity finally becomes. Cobb is rather impatient with a too facile and too definition-full understanding of "human nature." To treat " human nature" as though the concept has a perfectly clear and stable content is to ignore the vastly different ways that people have "got it together" as people since the first inklings of humanity at the dawn of psychic evolution. For example, the structure of human existence or experience of Neanderthal Man has little in common with the structure of twentieth century human experience. It may well have more in common, over all, with the structure of experience of pre-human primates. The classical concept of human nature does not make sufficient room for humankind's on-going creation of human history; human nature is still being created by human decisions that perpetuate *this* structure of existence rather than *that*, and which tomorrow can still make other decisions. Cobb feels that the different ways in which different cultures have perceived themselves and out of which they have structured their psychic experiences are simply too variant to yield an encompassing concept of "human nature." The Greek Socratic approach to life, for example, involves a great emphasis upon rationality in the structure of human experience. Rationality loomed large in the self-perception and self-understanding of that period. Persons for whom rationality is a dominant theme in self-understanding would easily experience emotional life as a "problem" since it does not always align itself with the rational.[112]

Cobb sees the structure of existence as manifested in the prophetic periods of Old Testament history as one in which the "ethical" is a central concern: responsibility of people before God, and the immediacy of God's concern with people's history. How the Old Testament Jews "got it together" differs drastically from how the Socratic Greeks "got it together."

The reason for this brief excursus on the structure of existence in a wide cultural sense is because Cobb maintains that such considerations have their analogue in the life of each person. There are certain perceptions which are central ones in our self-perception, and in our perception of the world; and those central perceptions are the keys to how we interpret experience. What persons mean when they say "I" derives largely from those central perceptions out of which they operate and around which they "get their life together." For example, a man's dominant way of understanding himself might be in terms of his role as husband; but that same man's life would "get put together" quite differently if his central perception of himself were in terms of mayor of the town, or of a hopeless failure! There is no way of weighing equally all those factors of our experience which contribute to the structure of our becoming. Some always emerge as dominant, which is to say that some contribute structurally much more than others, and that the dominant elements have a larger presence (affect more) in our psychic constitution.

Cobb then asks, "What was the central perception of Jesus?" When Jesus said "I," what was the structure of his experiencing that gave content to the meaning of his "I"? He writes that "God's presence in Jesus played a structural role in the actual occasions constituting his personal life which it has played nowhere else . . . He spoke on his own authority which was at the same time the authority of God. The 'I' of Jesus, rather than standing over and against the divine 'I', identified its authority with that of God. Among religious leaders of mankind, this is a unique role. . . It differs from the mystics and ecstatics as much as from the great Hebrew prophets. The 'I' of Jesus was neither merged with the divine nor replaced by the divine. On the contrary, it retained its autonomous existence, but in such a way as to identify its perceptions with God's. . . God's aim for Jesus was that he prehend God in terms of that which constitutes him as God — his Lordship, his love, and his incomparable superiority of being and value. This prehension was not experienced by Jesus as information about God but as the presence of God to and in him. Furthermore, and most uniquely, it was not experienced by him as one prehension alongside others to be integrated by him into a synthesis with them. Rather this prehension of God constituted in Jesus the center from which everything else in his psychic life was integrated. . . The 'I' of Jesus was constituted by his prehension of God.''[113]

Yet, the "self" or "I" of Jesus is marked by an unprecedented drive for breadth and inclusiveness. The "size" of the "self" of Jesus allowed him to work for self-actualization — not self-denial. The "me" of Jesus was not circumscribed by the outer edges of his skin surface; it was not merely a psychic self that animated a small portion of matter, i.e., his body. Jesus' "self" was his mode of presence in the world and the world's presence to him (the "field of force" imagery). The borders of the "self" of Jesus begin and end in God's initial aim and where his concern stops. For example, where were the borders of the world that had enough hold on Jesus to make him cry and die? Where were the last people located who could make him sad or happy? One implication of the *universal* love of Jesus is that the "I" of Jesus appropriated the destiny of everyone into his own self-hood.

The Christian claim is that God manifested his love for all in the Christ-Event. If that is true, then the happiness, for example, of Jesus needs the happiness of every human creature. Our lives in love are included in his life; and, at that point, our life is included in the definition of Jesus' "self." The self-realization of Jesus would therefore be inclusive of our responsive love. The "size" of the "self" of Jesus' love is therefore huge (agapé). The basic value stance of the Christ-Event in process thought is the stature of the "soul" of Jesus; the range and depth of his love and his capacity for relationships; the volume of life that he took into "self" and still maintained his integrity and individuality; the intensity and variety of outlook that he entertained in the unity of "self" without feeling defensive or insecure; the strength of his "spirit" that encouraged others to become freer in the development of their diversity and uniqueness; the "power" to sustain more complex and more enriching tensions; and the magnanimity of concern that he displayed to provide conditions that enabled others to increase in "stature." Access to "peak experiences" in the relationship of Jesus to God demanded this "size" of "self-hood"!

Another example of this "size" would be the statement of Gandhi that "as long as any person in the world lacks bread, I lack bread." The "self" of Gandhi here is co-extensive with humankind. When a "self" of that stature is operative, history is really delighted to have that kind of a "self" self-actualized — because everyone should benefit from it. Jesus, too, possessed tremendous inclusivity of "self." Jesus understood with blinding clarity that his own response to what the Father primordially called him to do required a "self" that was so huge that it was co-extensive with historical existence. This is why the historical Jesus could say: "Truly, I say to you, as you did it not to one of the least of these, you did it not to me." (Matthew 25:45)

At the practical level, from this perspective of "size," we might ask how bizarre is such a thing as the Mason-Dixon line!

Cobb's Christology therefore tries to offer conceptualization for Jesus' claim of the immediacy of God to his experience, to his very being. His Christology equally implies that, for some critical reason, what happened in and to Jesus is important for us today. That means that the Christian attempts to bring the Jesus-Event into frequent contact with his/her life and the life of the Church. The Jesus-Event and history engage each other in the on-goingness of daily reality. And only in the internality of that on-going moment can the Jesus-Event contribute to the configuration of history. But structures of responses to immediacies are too particular to enter into the structure of the *defining* characteristic. Two things happen where the Jesus-Event and contemporary history confront each other. One is that when we see the present version of what is going on in history, and then confront it with the Jesus-Event, we often find that we must try to re-shape history, i.e., take the version of it we have found, and do a reversion that is faithful to our understanding of Christian love. A second thing that happens when the Jesus-Event and history confront each other is that we often see the Jesus-Event in terms of the world view which our histories condition in us.

In a sense then, "each Christology is an historically conditioned version of the importance of Jesus. We are dealing here with the Whiteheadian category of 'conceptual reversion'."[114] A society, e.g., the Church, which wants to offer possibilities of intense life to its members must provide occasions and *dynamics* for the operation of the category of "conceptual reversion," i.e., it must make provision for contact between the Jesus-Event and immediate situations so that new appropriations of the Jesus-Event can be made in terms of the new challenges which history proffers.

A society, e.g., the Church, which wants to survive and to live intensely must constantly be on guard not to over-structure itself in its defining characteristics, because that can over-particularize the large sense of its meaning as a society. And it must also be careful not to get too detailed in whatever dynamisms it has to take care of "conceptual reversion," or else spontaniety in daily appropriations of the society's life-intuition will be hampered.

Dogmatic formulations are an attempt to capture somehow the essential kernel of a belief. They have often been imposed upon the entire Church with a definite sense of finality. Acceptance of such formulations has been understood to enter into the defining characteristics, for a person who did not accept them was anathema, i.e., outside the Church. The realization that every statement is historically conditioned, that every statement reflects certain presuppositions that derive from a world view, that every statement is *a* perspective — that realization should engender a reluctance to make content statements with finality.

Councils have been "essential to Church life from Nicaea to Vatican II not because of their positive doctrine but because of the linguistic conventions they established — ways of speaking which did not in themselves distort the faith and which provided a solid basis for further reflection as faith strove to deepen itself. These linguistic conventions imply that certain ways of speaking are true to the Jesus of the New Testament and other ways of speaking are not. (I believe that it is beyond question that the *intention* of all of the councils was to remain true to Scripture. The degree to which this was achieved was another question.) Their concern is to keep the real Jesus unchanged, to prevent the alteration or dissolution of his image by any of the popular or learned philosophies of the day. They do this, as they must, in making use of the language and conceptuality of precisely these popular and learned philosophies, and the formulas which they have left us make sense only in terms of this same language and conceptuality."[115]

The dangers seen by the councils are perennial in that human thought in every age will always try to domesticate Jesus. However, the councils are important also for what they did not achieve, i.e., their failure to break free of the immobile God which was the legacy of the Greek world, and to do this in the name of the *living* God who was their birthright. "Nature" and "substance," terms used frequently in dogma and theology, reflect basically that Greek world view. They are understandings that make eminent good sense within that framework. But what they have, in fact, done is impose a framework which is just *one* possible perspective. For example, the nature/person Christological formulation of Chalcedon and scholastic theology's "transubstantiation" explanation of the Eucharist so canonized a particular framework that new theology in a new framework became almost impossible.

Christianity even constitutes an almost insoluble problem for the Greek view of history, because Christianity is an historical faith. This faith asserts that God manifested himself once and for all in the unique historical event we know as Jesus the Christ. He is, in his unique historical individuality, God's "Word" to human persons in all centuries from the first through the twentieth to the end of time — but not process. Dwyer comments that "God spoke there and then and Christian faith is the believing reception of something which *happened* and therefore is still happening. To call Christianity an historical faith is to affirm that Christianity can never be 'dehistoricized', dissolved into a set of statements or doctrines above time and independent of history. It is the very *historicity* of Jesus — he transcended history by being involved in it and subject to it — which makes it so very difficult for Greek thought to cope with him. Faced with the New Testament evidence, the Greek mind will affirm the historical dimension of Jesus — that is, his humanity — as a *fact*, but it will always be at a loss in finding something for that humanity to do, and in attributing to it a real role in the saving of the human race.''[116] Only a divinized humanity could fulfill such a role for the Greek mind; and hence, the attraction of those theories in which in fact, if not in so many words, the humanity of Jesus is absorbed into the divinity.

A funny thing happened after the formula of Chalcedon. It was popularly assumed that the ''one person'' of Chalcedon was a Divine Person and an Eternal Son, two ideas the council had had nothing to say about. This *popular* orthodoxy carried the day against the guarded teaching of the council itself. So, the Second Council of Constantinople (553 C.E.) made this view specific, i.e., that the one person in Jesus is divine. The full *human* status of Jesus, God's ''son'' in the New Testament, ''has been maintained with difficulty ever since by this making the 'one person' of Chalcedon a divine person, something it did not say and the New Testament does not say. The closest the New Testament comes to Chalcedon is in portraying a man who is fully divine.''[117]

John Cobb (and many process thinkers) feels that such formulations must and should take place. But ''they pertain more to the *intensity* dynamism than to the *survival* dynamism. Formulations, because they are an attempt to come to grips with the Jesus-Event in terms of a particular perspective, are a matter of engagement of the Jesus-Event with ongoing history. That is an intensity dynamism. And no historically conditioned statement should be made to enter its contents into the defining characteristic of a Church which believes in its vocation to survive to the end of time.''[118]

The Church will always be articulating her self-understanding and will always be making historically conditioned statements. At this point, Cobb would want to remind the Church that its reality is its process, and that it would be better for the Church's survival potential to try to delineate its defining characteristics in *event* categories rather than substance categories. To say that faith in the importance of the Jesus-Event is a defining characteristic is to say very much, as long as ''importance'' is understood in the Whiteheadian sense. For it means that human life intends to take the Jesus-Event most seriously in the configuration of its own reality. The Jesus-Event — because it is ''important'' — provides occasions for future creative advance and the impetus for self-transcendence.

Cobb believes that in Jesus there is a revelation *par excellence* of the love of God and the design (Logos) of God. The events of the life and death of Jesus show a configuration of human life (a "structure of experience") responding fully to the summons of God. God touched history very powerfully in Jesus, and he continues the presence of that special appearance in the appropriation of the Jesus-Event in the life of the Church. The Church, "because it presents God to the world over and over again through a constant reappropriation of the Jesus-Event, is a reflection of God at work in the world; the Church is a sacrament of God at work in the world, especially through Jesus. The Church, like God, must issue man a summons of transcendence, a high hope of adventure; a quest and a hope and a promise. That summons operates above all in the structure of Christian love, as made explicit in the life of Jesus. A man . . . finds it difficult to love when love is not returned, for he cannot sustain such a negation. The Christian is specifically asked to sustain that negation, to absorb non-love — that is the meaning of the Cross."[119]

Lives-being-touched-by-Jesus is the process which constitutes the actuality of the Church. Bernard Lee phrases it this way: "the Christian emBodies the Church, and the Church emBodies the Christian. They are each other's life and self, not exhaustively but yet *really* and importantly."[120]

Perhaps it is enough to stress *that* the Jesus-Event is "important," i.e., that the Christian construes the meaning of his/her life and constructs its particular shape with the Jesus-Event as an important occasion of experience. A process model of understanding the Church suggests that the Church keep its own understanding of its defining characteristics in the largest terms possible. In other words, over-prescription in final and canonized formulations can easily inhibit the survival and intensity power of the society gathered around the event of Jesus. The structure of existence which "emBodies" Christian love, i.e., a love that has a deep conviction of people's intrinsic worth and which transcends differences and absorbs hatred, as well as a structure which has tried to refrain from very exacting specifications in its defining characteristics, ought to manifest a rather strong pluralism in its membership.[121]

This approach to Christology sees Jesus less as a revelation of *what* humankind is (though something of that too), and more as a revelation of *how* process goes at its heart, a "how" that Christian love supports and reinforces, a "how" that lets humans become all that they can become.

Cobb maintains that "Jesus brought into being for those who responded to him a final and unsurpassable structure of existence . . . In its turn, however, it has introduced new possibilities of sickness and fragmentation as well as new possibilities of health."[122] But how (by what criteria) the quality of life achieved by Jesus within the structure of existence in his situation is to be translated into the "final and unsurpassable structure of existence" opened by Jesus for the Christian in his radically different situation is never disclosed by Cobb.[123] And the quotation given immediately above also poses the question: isn't that contradictory? How (in the context of the Kingdom motif) is it possible for what is allegedly a "final and unsurpassable structure of existence" to pose "new possibilities of sickness and fragmentation?" asks Carpenter.[124] If this is the case, does it not follow that there must be some other structure of existence which could surpass our supposedly "final and unsurpassable structure of existence?"

Has not Cobb created a possible conflict between our prehensions of Jesus and our prehensions of God? There are other aims at one's fulfillment, and among them is the inheritance from past actual occasions in some other living person. But Cobb is apparently not concerned whether this inheritance is from the immediate or the remote past. If this is so, what is there to prevent a conflict between the aim at our fulfillment from Jesus and the ideal aim from God? Must we either devalue Jesus' aim at our fulfillment in maximizing the route of inheritance from God or devalue the ideal aim from God should we choose to maximize what Jesus would afford us? All of these questions are posed for Cobb by James Carpenter.[125]

With the assistance of Bernard Lee (as cited above), we hope that some of Carpenter's misconceptions of Cobb's Christology have already been defused. But Cobb himself has not let Carpenter's observations go by without a careful rebuttal. He observes that

Carpenter really equates his "structure of existence" with "quality of life," which was not his intention.[126] It is not contradictory for Cobb to speak of a "structure of existence as unsurpassable" and also state that it introduces new types of evil. Carpenter misinterprets this because he sees that "structure of life" as life with superior quality in which these new types of evil are overcome. Carpenter seems to use "quality of life" as an ethical concept. "My interest," writes Cobb, "on the other hand, is to show that historical 'progress' has not led to greater and greater virtue or improved quality of life but to greater possibilities for good and evil. Axial existence is productive of far greater good and far greater evil than primitive existence. Jesus had an immense effect on human history both in calling forth a new structure of existence capable to the highest degree of both good and evil *and* in helping to overcome the evil."[127]

Cobb is insistent that here at least he dealt with intrapsychic structures rather than the relations of one occasion to other entities. The finality he claimed for Christian existence had to do only with intrapsychic structures, so that "in the relationship to God, which distinguished Jesus from us, we are to hope for something quite different from what we now know."[128]

The notion of "presence" in process categories might be of some assistance here. For example, the conventional concept of "presence" might be interpreted so that each student attending my class lecture is present to me. But my wife is "absent" — because she is shopping in New York City. However, at the second-thought level of process, the concept of "presence" will be providing me with another answer. If I try to account to you about who "I" am, about the people and the events that are "present" in my life, I will really be re-counting the people and events that are most *influencing* me right now. If I hardly know my students (even though we might be in the same room), the case will be that my wife in New York City has far more *power* over my life than my students have. The principal notion of "presence" in process thought, therefore, is how much power one has over our lives — not how close together we might be either spatially or temporally. My wife affects me more, is more present! The "density" of her "presence" affects me more and shapes me more. Analogously, the Jesus-Event of one historical time and space can yield more *power* over the life of the contemporary Christian — and, therefore, there will be a denser presence of that Event trans-historically and trans-culturally.

"Presence" finally means having effects. The "presence" of the Jesus-Event can shape the life of the Christian in the twentieth century in some significant way. The event of Jesus is "present" today to the Christian because it has a hold on his/her becoming; it alters his/her present personal configuration. The Jesus-Event in process categories is "present" because it takes some of its configuration and gives it to the Christian of this era for his/her configuration — the Christian says "Yes" to that event and builds it into his/her self. "Presence" is a function of an event in process conceptuality.

In **A Christian Natural Theology** Cobb specified quite unequivocally that only God is to be identified with this "aim at universal intensity of satisfaction"[129] or principle of guidance in the universe. He alone is "the ground of being, the ground of purpose, and the ground of order"[130] which makes possible and sustains the ongoing existence of each of us within the context of the larger purposes which all our existence together ultimately are to serve and to which they must constantly be redirected.[131]

Cobb does indicate that his Whiteheadian Christology is an attempt to resolve the classical problem for theology of how to account for God's unique presence in Jesus without displacement of any aspect of Jesus' humanity.[132] In the light of his views concerning the providential guidances of God and the dynamics of the relationship between God and Jesus, James Carpenter claims that Cobb's contention that Jesus is both the ground of the "final and unsurpassable structure of existence" which he introduced and "the one in relation to whom the health of that structure can be attained"[133] is a case either of unnecessary duplication or of outright conflict between Jesus and God which attributes to Jesus a role elsewhere assigned by Cobb exclusively to God.[134]

Cobb counters Carpenter's misunderstanding in which he finds conflict or redundancy in the influence Cobb attributes to Jesus and to God. He maintains that if all influences on a human occasion were to be identified with direct influence upon aims then Carpenter's observation would be accurate. But "the dominant efficacy of the past upon us is not directly a contribution to our aims. In Whitehead's presentation there is a marked difference between the causal efficacy of the past and the derivation of the initial aim from God."[135]

In other words, past occasions do affect the present aim in that the initial aim is always relevant to the concrete situation of the concrescing occasion (its actual world), which is the totality of these past occasions. That is not a conflict in Cobb's interpretation. *Both* the causal efficacy of past occasions and new possibilities derived from God are metaphysically required.

Consequently, Cobb declares that there is "no redundancy between the efficacy of past persons, including Jesus, and the efficacy of God. We live in a very different world because of Jesus, and for that reason we derive very different aims from God than we would derive if we were not in Jesus' sphere of influence. In part, Jesus' influence is to sensitize us to God's graciousness and thus to inspire trust in the initial aim. To be deeply affected by Jesus is to become more receptive to God's aim for us. . . . His efficacy is to be seen primarily in the new structure of existence he called into being. . . . The teaching of Jesus, combined with the experience of the earliest community of believers, led to the emergence of the Christian structure."[136]

To recapitulate, we will put Pittenger and Cobb in a "theological blender" to see what emerges. Process theology says that, in general, God acts by providing an ideal aim for every situation in which we find ourselves. We then respond to that ideal aim, and more or less actualize it. So, every human situation has a dual component: there is an ideal aim for that situation, and there is our actualization of that aim to a greater or lesser degree. This is how God acts in general in the world. If we use these categories, how then do we understand who Jesus is? First of all, Jesus is the person for whom God's ideal aim was that he, in his life, death and resurrection, totally express the nature of God and God's relationship to humankind. Jesus was not only the person for whom God had this extraordinarily high ideal aim, but he was the person who responded totally in his human freedom to that ideal aim — and therefore, in this perfect match of ideal aim and human response, came revelation. So: Jesus is *different in kind* (because God's ideal aim for him is much different than God's ideal aim for the rest of us), and he is *different in degree* (because Jesus totally responded to his ideal aim and we more or less respond, i.e., we are always in a situation of generosity in response and always in a situation of resistance and denial).

Therefore, process theology, using the categories of ideal aim and subjective response, explores faith and the richness of who Jesus was and is so that we can more deeply understand him.

This leads us now to Cobb's further process Christological elaborations in **Christ in a Pluralistic Age.**

IV. CHRIST AS CREATIVE TRANSFORMATION
AND TILLICH'S "NEW BEING"

John Cobb's developing Christology is explored in his book entitled **Christ in a Pluralistic Age.**[137] In his Introduction, he maintains that "much that we have meant by Christ in the past, when we did not acknowledge pluralism, becomes destructive in our new situation. If Christ means the absolutization of one pattern of life against others, then Christ is . . . in opposition to our real need today. . . . Christ, as the image of creative transformation, can provide a unity within which the many centers of meaning and existence can be appreciated and encouraged and through which openness to the other great Ways of mankind can lead to a deepening of Christian experience."[138]

Cobb contends that his proposal can be clarified in relation to a well-known formulation of Paul Tillich. Tillich pointed out that "the human problem has been experienced variously in different periods of Christian history, and that accordingly the meaning of Christ as the answer also changes . . . These are all contrasted by Tillich with Luther's doctrine of justification by faith and his own idea of the New Being in Jesus as the Christ that overcomes[139] 'disruption, conflict, self-destruction, meaninglessness and despair in all realms of life.' "[140]

This process of change did not end with Tillich — and indeed the process has been accelerated. Today, says Cobb, "the basic human question is no longer exclusively or primarily existential. . . . The question the Christian hears . . . is whether there is a way through the chaos of our time so that we can be brought together with others rather than try to run roughshod over them. This book proposes that for us Christ is the Way that excludes no Ways. Tillich by no means intended to deny continuity and unity to Christ. No more do I. He believed that the New Being is the answer in every human situation. Similarly, to understand Christ as creative transformation illuminates also the creative transformation of Christ himself through which he answers the changing needs of human history without ceasing to be one and the same Christ."[141]

Our task here will be to compare and perhaps even reconcile

Tillich's ontological concept of the New Being as Jesus the Christ with Cobb's Whiteheadian construction of Christ as the image of creative transformation.

Paul Tillich uses the contemporary category of existentialist ontology to try to understand who Jesus is for us. His basic vision of the human person is that of a sinful condition, i.e., he/she is estranged. And this estrangement in sin has a three-fold dynamic. First of all, it is unbelief, i.e., a turning away from God; and in this turning away from God, the second element of estrangement begins to be seen. It is *hubris* (or pride), a turning toward the self; a deep involvement with the self; a centering of self in the ego. And in that moment of the centering of the self in the ego, the third element of the dynamic of one human person's estrangement becomes evident. It is concupiscence, i.e., the unlimited desire to protect the self at all costs. There is no end to this; but it is constantly pursued.

For Tillich, this estranged situation of the human person basically leads to "idolatry."[142] He means that we take something that is finite and conditioned and we invest it with infinity and unconditionedness. We ask some finite object to be "God" for us: another person to secure our futures, wealth, prestige, fame, religious nationalism, etc. — and they cannot. The human person therefore is estranged from God and then demonically centered in self; we continually invest objects with God-hood that they might save us from our plight because we cannot do it ourselves; we cannot extricate ourselves from this estranged situation.

Tillich makes clear that the term "God" is unsoundly used if it designates only a deity with whom persons can live comfortably, without tension. He writes that "a man who has never tried to flee God has never experienced the God Who is really God. . . . For there is no reason to flee a god who is the perfect picture of everything that is good in man . . . who is simply the universe, or the laws of nature, or the course of history . . . who is nothing more than a benevolent father, a father who guarantees our immortality and final happiness. Why try to escape from someone who serves us so well? No, those are not pictures of God, but rather of man, trying to make God in his own image and for his own comfort."[143]

Historically, the search for wholeness over against estrangement in human existence has found expression chiefly in the religious life of humankind. The religious concern, says Tillich, is "ultimate, unconditioned, total, and infinite."[144] Even the experience of meaninglessness involves the assumption that life claims to be significant: some belief in meaning or its possibility is the point of reference. Tillich has penetratingly commented that even doubt and despair express the meaning in which the doubter and the desperate are still living.[145] He writes that "this unconditional seriousness is the expression of the presence of the divine in the experience of their separation from it."[146]

Tillich can even describe the confrontation with the threat of non-being in terms of "ontological shock," in which the mind reaches its boundary and is thrown off balance, "shaken in its structures." However, what is experienced is "the negative side of the mystery of being — its absysmal element."[147] Thus the experience of the shock of non-being actually produces a consciousness of the power of being. Indeed, Tillich regards this negative element as necessary for revelation, since without it mystery would not be mysterious. Without Isaiah's awareness of being "undone", his vision of God would have been impossible. Apart from "the dark night of the soul", the mystic could not experience the mystery of the "ground of being."[148]

Tillich's view of God as the "ground of being" makes clear that the depth or ground of history (which he identifies with God) is nothing inert or fixed. It is rather "infinite and inexhaustible."[149] It is both source and aim of our life in society and of what claims our unreserved commitment in ethical and political action.[150]

This is the existential situation as seen by Tillich. Who, then, is Jesus? Jesus is the New Being who comes under the conditions of existence. He is *essential* "God-manhood" as we are distorted "God-manhood", i.e., "God-manhood" that is not in right relationship. But Jesus is *essential* "God-manhood", "God-manhood" that is in right relationships. He is New Being (not like our being that is distorted and estranged) but he comes under the conditions of Old Being, i.e., to use mythological terms, he comes into the sinful world and suffers the sins of that world in order that we might be redeemed, that we might have contact with New Being. In these terms of existential ontology then, Jesus the Christ is seen as the New Being. This, for Tillich, is a symbolic theological expression of faith that God (the transcendent mystery of all that is) is uniquely known and encountered in the personal event of Jesus the Christ.

As the summary of his ministry in the Fourth Gospel, Jesus cries out and says: "He who believes in me, believes not in me but in him who sent me. And he who sees me sees him who sent me." (John 12:44ff.) Jesus, that is to say, reveals God by being utterly *transparent* to him, precisely as he is nothing "in himself." Tillich makes this the criterion of the whole Christian claim that Jesus is. the final revelation of God.[151] He writes that "the question of the final revelation is the question of a medium of revelation which overcomes its own finite conditions by sacrificing them, and itself with them. He who is the bearer of the final revelation must surrender his finitude — not only his life but also his finite power and knowledge and perfection. In doing so, he affirms that he is the bearer of final revelation (the 'Son of God' in classical terms). He became completely transparent to the mystery he reveals. But, in order to be able to surrender himself completely, he must possess himself completely. And only he can possess — and therefore surrender — himself completely who is united with the ground of his being and meaning without separation and disruption. In the picture of Jesus as the Christ we have the picture of a man who possesses these qualities, a man who, therefore, can be called the medium of final revelation."[152]

Mention should be made here of Tillich's methodology — the method of correlation. Tillich could not tolerate the sharp separation between theology and culture upon which Barth and other Neo-orthodox theologians were insisting. He felt that the theologian must first listen attentively to the questions of human existence buried in the temporal situation and *then* respond with the power of the timeless message. This is what Tillich calls *"apologetic" or "answering theology,"* a theology which seeks to find the common ground between the message and the situation by listening first to the questions posed before answering in terms of the Christian message.

Tillich, therefore, does not make revelation or its contents the starting point of his theology, but rather begins with humankind. Theology should satisfy two basic needs: the statement of the truth of the Christian message and the interpretation of that message for every new generation. Theology then moves between two poles; namely, the eternal truth of its foundation and the temporal situation in which this truth must be received. Therefore, for Tillich, kerygmatic theology (the message of revelation with the emphasis on the unchangeable truth of the message) requires apologetic ("answering") theology for its completion.[153]

The first formal criterion, which distinguishes theology from every other discipline, is stated by Tillich in this fashion: "the object of theology is what concerns us ultimately. Only those propositions are theological which deal with their object in so far as it can become a matter of ultimate concern for us."[154] "Ultimate concern" is the "abstract translation" of the great commandment: "The Lord our God, the Lord is one; and you shall love the Lord your God with all your heart; and with all your soul, and with all your mind and with all your strength." (Deut. 6: 4-5) The content of this "ultimate concern" is that which is most important to humankind; namely, that without which he/she is not — *his/her being*. The "ultimate concern" of humankind is that which has the power to destroy or save this being. This term, for Tillich — the term "being" — does not designate existence in time or space in the present context. It means the whole of human reality, the structure, meaning and aim of existence. All this is threatened and can be either saved or lost. Tillich comments that " 'to be or not to be' in this sense is a matter of ultimate, unconditional, total and infinite concern."[155]

Tillich asserts that apologetic theology is to "show that trends immanent in all religions and cultures move toward the Christian answer."[156] Only Christianity can deal with real "ultimate concern." Nothing can be ultimate unless it can be *universal* and absolute; yet nothing can be a concern which is not *concrete* and existential. For this reason only in Christian theology where the Logos became flesh is there offered the absolutely universal and the asolutely concrete theology which is the adequate object of "ultimate concern."

The question that must be asked is this: what is the criterion according to which the theologian chooses and judges both the sources of theology and his/her experiences that mediate the sources. It is the contention of Tillich that in the early Church the *material* norm was the Creed, and the *formal* norm was the hierarchical authorities guarding the "deposit" of revelation. Later on, the formal norm predominated. The Reformers asserted the material norm to be justification by faith and the formal norm to be the Bible. Tillich obviously feels that the present generation requires a new expression of the norm of theology, a norm which will express the situation of our times; a situation which can be described in terms of estrangement, disruption, conflict, self-destruction, meaninglessness, and despair in all realms of life. The question arising from such a situation is the question of a reality in which self-estrangement is overcome, a reality of reconciliation and reunion, of creativity, meaning and hope. This reality Tillich calls the *New Being*; and this "New Being" is present and realized in Jesus the Christ, whose power is triumphant over the demonic separations of the old order of reality. Consequently, the most authentic and adequate norm for contemporary theology is then "the New Being in Jesus as the Christ as our ultimate concern."[157]

To recapitulate: the norm for Tillich's theology is "the New Being in Jesus as the Christ as our ultimate concern." It is produced in the life of the Church, derived from the Bible, conditioned by culture, and made to "come alive" by experience.[158]

Tillich employs also what he calls *"the Protestant principle,"* i.e., the rule that all finite expressions of humankind's experience of God must finally be denied, or else they will become idolatrous distortions, and that only in their self-denial can they affirm God. Tillich, therefore, feels himself free to make use of all the materials provided by Church history without being bound in any way by them.[159]

This discussion above has seemed, among other things, to be a case study in Tillich's methodology of correlation. Truths from the philosophical existential situation and Christian theology encounter one another to the end that "questions" raised about human existence, e.g., "Do I have the courage to be?", were *correlated* with the "answers" of revelation. Tillich himself sums it up this way: "The method of correlation explains the contents of the Christian faith through existential questions and theological answers in mutual interdependence.''[160] The answers of revelation have meaning only if correlated with questions relative to our existence as finite creatures. And we can get the ultimate answer to our questions only in revelatory events. Question and answer must intersect and interpenetrate.

Finite persons enjoy an *essential* unity with the infinite, so they are *able* to ask about the infinite to which they belong. However, they are simultaneously separated *existentially* from the infinite, so they are *compelled* to ask about the infinite. Even if the answer has to be in some way reformulated, Tillich is convinced that nothing he sees can change the *substance* of the answer, inasmuch as this substance is the Logos of being manifested in Jesus as the Christ. Theological answers extract their *content* from revelation; they draw their *form* from the questions of existence.[161]

There are some Christian thinkers besides Barth who take sharp issue with Tillich's methodology. For example, the American-Swedish theologian Nels F.S. Ferré, who has always had high respect for Tillich, maintains that Tillich's position cannot be held within the Christian faith without fundamentally altering and destroying it. Ferré states very emphatically that "in intellectual honesty a person is Christian or Tillichian, but he cannot be both."[162] And George H. Tavard, a Roman Catholic theologian who upholds the Christological teaching of the Council of Chalcedon as the norm for both Catholic and Protestant christians, calls Tillich's Christology deficient because "it is not so much focused on a historical event (the actual coming of Christ in human form) as on a philosophico-religious principle."[163]

Recently, however, Gerald O'Collins, S.J., has sketched some major concerns and challenges that have consistently shown up in the serious Jesus literature over the last decade. He writes that "it has been widely agreed that Christian belief about Jesus' personal identity and redemptive functions should be correlated with human experiences, questions, sufferings and hopes . . . (after Bultmann) Paul Tillich used his method of correlation to link our existential alienation and self-destructiveness with the new being offered by Jesus as the Christ . . . Pierre Teilhard de Chardin (also) . . . in its 'Pastoral Constitution on the Church in the Modern World'

(1965), the Second Vatican Council encouraged the method of correlation by presenting the redemptive revelation brought by Christ
in terms of the deep questions thrown up by human life itself.
. . . Whether they explicitly state this or not, through the 1970's
into the 1980's professional theologians and church leaders have
frequently maintained and updated the method of correlation
[O'Collins then cites the works of Rahner, Schillebeeckx, Kasper,
Sobrino, Panikkar, and Dhavamony] . . . Pope John Paul II's
'Catechesi Tradendae,' an apostolic exhortation on catechetics
(October 16, 1979), tended to encourage the same method of correlation in presenting the mystery of Christ . . . there is no need
to decide between a historical approach to Christology and the more
philosophical method of correlation. We are not dealing with two
separate authorities: some specific *historical* events concerning Jesus
as experienced, witnessed to and recorded by the first Christians
and the common experience of primordial human questions, needs
and hopes that can be interpreted and clarified *philosophically* for
their general significance. We should not oppose a 'historical
authority' (the once-and-for-all experience of God in Jesus of
Nazareth) to a 'philosophical authority' (the deep and universally
relevant concerns that faith in Christ promises to satisfy today).
In the particular we find the universal: Jesus is the Christ. . . .
Redemption does not mean escaping from this material creation,
but its ultimate transformation.''[164] (italics added)

One further corollary here might be beneficial prior to our attempt
to see if there can be any theological coherence between Tillich and
John Cobb. Some consideration will be given to the use of "symbols" and symbolic language. First of all, Tillich's basic definition
of God is that he is being-itself,[165] not *a* being, not even *a* being
above all others. God as being-itself is beyond space and substance,
essence and existence. "Being-itself" is a very critical term for Tillich
because it signifies the "power inherent in everything, the power
of resisting non-being."[166] "Being-itself" and "power of being"
are the two terms for God which Tillich uses. A third term, made
popular by Bishop John A.T. Robinson in his **Honest to God**, is
"ground of being." Robinson drew upon a much-quoted Tillich
sermon, "The Depth of Existence."[167]

Tillich wants us to grasp that all things that are rest upon being-itself, upon God, as their ground. There is though only *one* non-symbolic statement about God: God is "being-itself." We have already seen that in the method of correlation, Christian symbols must always be correlated with existential questions; but existential questions are ontological ones, so the answers must be ontological as well. And the only way to express humankind's "Ultimate concern" is through symbols. Symbolic language alone is capable of unveiling the ultimate. In brief, Christian theology presents Christian symbols in ontological terms.

It is rumored that Tillich used to get very agitated if someone used the expression "*merely* a symbol." For him, symbols have power to open up levels of reality which previously have been closed; symbols do something to us, i.e., they can unlock dimensions and elements *within us* which correspond to the dimensions and elements of reality. Symbols also develop out of the individual or collective unconscious; they cannot be produced arbitrarily. And symbols grow when the situation is ripe for them; they die when they can no longer produce a response in the group where they originally found expression.[168] All subsequent statements about God as "being-itself" will be symbolic. Tillich's intention is to signify by the one non-symbolic statement that God is the ground of the ontological structure of being without becoming in any way subordinate to the structure. Every true symbol points beyond itself to something else and it participates in the reality which it symbolizes.[169]

Secondly, the notion of "symbol" in process modes of thought must be examined. "*Transmutation*" is a process theological concept and it is part of every encounter that takes place between any two actual entities. One actual entity can never take into its experience the whole of another actual entity in all of its entirety; only some aspects, or perhaps even a single aspect. For example, there is no way that one person can encounter another person in his/her totality, i.e., in the fullness of his/her mystery and in every element of his/her history. We pick out one or another salient feature or characteristic of another person; we pick out some limited number of things about another person and let them serve as our "handles." Transmutation, therefore, means the way that one actual entity *simplifies* another actual entity in order to experience it. It is the way we get "handles" on our experience; a part which mediates the experience of the whole, i.e., data is simplified through a partial selection. (Another word for transmutation is "focus.") As soon as a person "focuses" on one thing, then other things go to the periphery, and other things just disappear completely. Transmutation, therefore, is *simplification* that is necessarily a part of every transaction or interaction between actual entities.

To progress a bit further: the concept of "symbol" in process thought is very closely related to "transmutation." For when a transmutation is brought to the level of consciousness in human life we are speaking of a symbol. For example, Paul, prior to his conversion, was in "the field of force" of the Jesus-Event in a *negative* manner. In his dramatic moment of conversion however, he accepted in a *positive* manner the Jesus-Event in his "field of force." Once he did that, Paul began to interact with the Jesus-Event. Then he began to look at what that interaction did to his life; he reflects on it *after* it happened. And he begins to realize that it made a "new man" out of him; he begins to realize that that encounter with the Jesus-Event brought him "new being"; and he begins to realize that Jesus could do that because he himself was a "new man." Paul knew that Jesus "did humanity" in some new ways. Paul then saw that there were things in his life that were there in the Jesus-Event, and he knew that they got into his life derivatively from the Jesus-Event. Consequently, it was very easy and natural for him to speak about the Jesus-Event in terms of "new man," "new being," "new creation" — these were his "handles" for the Jesus-Event. Paul transmutated the Jesus-Event through *symbols* like that. The "first man" who attempted to "do humanity" was Adam; and somebody else attempted to do a brand new version of being human. Paul sees that in Jesus and in his own life, so that now it is especially easy for him to call Jesus a "Second Adam." The event of Jesus has now been transmutated through certain symbols.

Another example: the author (authors) of the Fourth Gospel experienced the Jesus-Event as Paul did, and was in "the field of force" of the Jesus-Event. But the Jesus-Event apparently impacted somewhat differently on the author of the Fourth Gospel than it did on Paul. Therefore, when he gets excited about the Jesus-Event he uses language such as "Light" or "Truth." The author of the Fourth Gospel is excited about this Jesus who takes something about God out of concealment and discloses it.

What is happening here is that there were different transmutations in the interaction of the author of the Fourth Gospel with the Jesus-Event than of Paul with the Jesus-Event, so that, when each of them "grabs hold" of the Jesus-Event by "handles," the "handles" that they get are "handles" from the way the Jesus-Event impacted upon their lives. There is complementarity here and not contradiction. All of the Pauline and Johannine texts alluded to here have a really different slant — and each creates a different *mood*. A Christian, for example, who would be shaped almost entirely by the Pauline "symbols" would have a different *flavor* than a Christian shaped by the Johannine "symbols." One isn't right; the other wrong. The important point here is that different symbols have different effects.

Therefore, in process thought, the symbols which function as our "handles" on an event shape the impact of that event on the human person. For example, it may be that when one person experiences another, what they really find attractive and "focus" in on about the other person is his/her complete candor in every situation. That candor then becomes a major symbol by which the one person knows the other. The one person is then influenced by the other; by being around that very candid person and letting that candid person have power over him/her, he/she finds it much easier to be really frank. The symbol ("candor"), which has mediated the experience of the other person, shapes the conversational partner. The forms of a person's definition stand a chance of becoming the forms of another person's definition also.

In human consciousness, therefore, symbols are involved in every act of presence. There are not some kinds of presence that are direct and some kinds of presence that are symbolic. Every act of presence involves symbolism because they always have to have some "handles" through which we can grab hold of our experiences of others or of some event. Symbols are always involved in our access to other persons and events.

Symbols are the way in which the Jesus-Event becomes present or is transmutated. A symbol, therefore, discloses a fuller reality than itself, and the basis for disclosure is that the symbol really participates in what it discloses. The mediating symbols of every conscious human transaction shape the power one entity has over another.[170]

* * * * *

Whitehead's philosophy is one of the very few contemporary comprehensive theories that is necessarily theistic in its implications. Using that philosophical construction as foundational, John B. Cobb, Jr. offers another "essay" in his foray into Christological concentration in **Christ in a Pluralistic Age**.[171]

By Christ Cobb means not just Jesus but *any* incarnation of the Word or Logos of God. Since the Logos is identified with God's primordial nature, i.e., with the totality of the possibilities God envisages for the world, its incarnation is seen in the actualization of any radically new and creative possibilities derived from God, and that actualization must result in "creative transformation." On this account, incarnation is radically *generalized*, and the specialness of Jesus must be explained in another way.

Cobb's thesis would maintain that there are many different kinds of human subjectivity. He therefore proposes that the specific center of Jesus' subjectivity is constituted by the divine Logos. This position is rather close to the Chalcedonian formula — for Cobb sees God as present in Jesus only objectively.

Cobb argues that Christians must be open to the possibility of radical creative transformation in the light of the insights of other religious traditions. His contention is based on analogy with Malraux's study of the image of Christ in the history of art, showing how it must lose itself in other traditions in order to find itself. In doing so, incarnation now no longer clearly means the actualization of God's novel possibilities as the effective embodiment of these aims in religious images that can capture the allegiance of people. In this way Cobb can encompass the richly symbolic and not merely abstractly conceptual nature of other religious traditions, e.g., Buddhism.

The image of Christ, particularly when Jesus is interpreted in Chalcedonian terms, does not necessarily entail such transformation the way in which incarnation as the actualization of divine novel aims does. The Chalcedonian formula was perhaps necessary if Jesus was the *only* incarnation of the Logos, but it may well complicate things for a more universal conceptualization of Christ.

Buddhism has dissolved Brahman into Emptiness, while a similar dissolution of Being has taken place at the hands of Heidegger and Whitehead (creativity). Instead of their identity, the two new ultimates, God and creativity, are both now affirmed as incommensurable — and this is used by Cobb as a means of appreciating positively the quest of Buddhism.[172]

More specifically, Cobb's thesis is that "faithfulness to Christ requires immersion in the secular and pluralistic consciousness and that it is precisely there that Christ now works, impeded by our failures to recognize him and by our continuing association of faith with past, particularized expressions of Christ."[173] He argues for this thesis by seeking to show that the very process that has produced and is at work in the secular and pluralistic consciousness is the process "creative transformation" that is properly named "Christ." He will not allow the image of Christ to be exclusive of secularity and pluralism. Instead, Cobb proposes to re-establish Christian faith by holding that Christ, in reality, is their own "basis" or "positive principle."[174]

Although the objective study of religion breaks "the correlation of faith and the sacred" and relativizes all absolutized particulars, the Christian not only can accept these consequences but should also affirm them. For "the remaining absolute" necessarily presupposed by objective study itself is "creative transformation as such," and the Christian should recognize that just that is the present working of Christ.[175]

Cobb seeks to discern the reality of Christ in the present as creative transformation, which he interprets in broadly Whiteheadian terms as "the universal presence of the transcendent Logos."[176] He then turns from the present to the past in order to consider "Christ as

Jesus," and attempts to ground the process of creative transformation historically in "Jesus and his influence."[177] Both encounter with the words of Jesus and incorporation into the field of his influence effect creative transformation in the hearer, the reason for this being that the Logos which is universally present as creative transformation "was distinctly embodied in Jesus," who was its "full incarnation."[178] Cobb draws here upon a distinction made by Whitehead as regards the relationality of all things. There is a "huge" sense of relationality — and, on the other hand, we realize that the world that actually does touch us is much smaller (not just spatially), the world of events from history. There are some historical events that shape us tremendously, but there are billions of events from the past that barely touch us. Therefore, there is a difference between the *whole* world (which means everything) and the *actual* world (which means that part of the whole world which is effectively our context). Cobb equates this with the expression "field of force." For example, a Christian's life can be described as experience in which the Jesus-Event is one of the large components in the actual world of a person. A Christian is someone whose "field of force" owns the Jesus-Event in a significant way; he/she "ingests" that Event.

Cobb also considers Christ in relation to the future. He argues that the distinctive structure of existence that was embodied in Jesus unifies four contemporary images of hope into "one immanent/transcendent, personal/communal, human/cosmic hope."[179] Cobb presents a meaningful constructive interpretation of the constitutive Christological assertion that "Jesus is the Christ."[180] He states that human beings embody many structures of existence which "are correlated with different roles of the Logos. . ."[181] In all but one of these structures, they constitute themselves around a center that is distinct from God's presence in them."[182] Nevertheless, one structure of existence is at least possible (theoretically) in which "the presence of the Logos would share in constituting selfhood[183] . . . the "I" in each moment (would be) constituted as much in the subjective reception of the lure to self-actualization that is the call and presence of the Logos as it (would be) in continuity with the personal past. This structure of existence would be the incarnation of the Logos in the fullest meaningful sense."[184] This distinctive structure of existence was actually embodied in Jesus due to the historical "datum" of Jesus' implicit claim to authority. There was a belief on the part of his disciples (based on the biblical witness) that Jesus was not continuously free from the tension between his "I" and the Logos.[185] But "at least at important times in his life Jesus freely chose to constitute his own selfhood as one with the presence of God within him."[186] Any understanding of Christ must be grounded in the historical Jesus.[187]

As mentioned earlier, Cobb means by "Christ" *any* incarnation of the Word or Logos of God — not just Jesus. The specialness of Jesus in the perspective of Christianity must therefore be explained in a different manner. Cobb's thesis is that there are many different kinds of human subjectivity responsive to the Logos or the primordial nature of God. In the case of Jesus, the specific center of his subjectivity was constituted by the divine Logos in that Jesus actualized all the radically new and creative possibilities derived from the initial aims of God's primordial nature. Cobb's hypothesis is that "in Jesus there appeared in an important way a structure of existence of whose occurrence elsewhere we have no evidence. It follows from this hypothesis that the difference between Jesus and Christian believers is not a matter of degree but one of kind, i.e., participation in different structures of existence."[188] The question must be asked then: "How close is this position to the Chalcedonian formula?" Robert E. Doud has attempted a synthesis of Karl Rahner and John Cobb by arguing on Rahner's behalf for two subjects in Jesus, one divine and one human, while Cobb sees God as present in Jesus only objectively. Doud would try to bridge this difference by his notion of "the transference of subjectivity" — a very complex idea, to say the least.[189]

Cobb's focus of interest here is a constructive answer to the question of how God can be affirmed to have been fully incarnate in Jesus. But, as Schubert M. Ogden has detected, there are considerable incidences of confusing, if not confused, formulations, which in some cases seem to reflect real inconsistencies in thought.[190] For example, Cobb can say at one time that "Jesus is Christ, because he is the incarnation of the Logos,"[191] even though, by his own

88

account, the Logos is *universally* incarnate (at least in all living beings and human persons), and *Jesus* is the Christ because he is the "full" or "fullest" incarnation of the Logos.[192]

Again, and even more seriously, Cobb can assume in one place that "the study of the many faith stances correlated with the many forms of the sacred has permanently eroded them all," and yet propose in another place that the Christian faith stance can now "re-establish itself" as "the basis for the objective study that breaks the correlation of faith and the sacred."[193] How can the same faith stance both be "permanently eroded" by, and also "re-establish itself" as the "basis" for, the objective study of religions? Also, is the theological change now called for simply to endorse the secular struggle to become free from the sacred?[194] Or, on the other hand, is the theological change now called for simply to relocate the sacred, and therefore affect a "transference of commitment" from "every form in which Christ has previously been known" to the process of creative transformation that is the reality of Christ itself?[195]

John Cobb responds to these criticisms with remarkable conciseness. He writes: "I want to argue *both* that our relation to our own tradition (the correlation of our faith with what has been recognized by this tradition as sacred) is broken *and* that when we recognize that the break was itself faithful, faith in a new sense is possible. . . . I am calling for the embracing of 'scientific' or 'objective' study of Christianity along with other religions, a form of study that distances us from what is studied in a way that is opposed to what we have meant by 'faith.' I am arguing that in a deeper sense this distancing expresses faith and that we need to recognize as Christ that in which this faith is placed. Hence I want to say both that what we have known as faith is dead and also that affirmation of this death is a new form of faith in broken continuity with the old."[196]

Ogden is extremely complimentary when he states that Cobb's "basic proposal for re-establishing Christian faith in a pluralistic age strongly commends itself to me. . . . I find what he says about the universal, if largely anonymous, working of Christ and about the meaning of Christian hope both illumining and provocative. Particularly significant, in my opinion, is his comparative discussion of the Christian and Buddhist structures of existence and of the present possibilities of each creatively transforming the other."[197]

After this very gracious commendation though, Ogden states that "there is Cobb's astonishing anti-Whiteheadian claim that 'in fact [our own achievements] are not our own achievements at all but achievements of the Logos in which we have actively participated'."[198] Ogden feels that this claim is implicitly, at least, self-contradictory: for either we *have* "actively participated" in the Logos' achievements (in which case they *are* our achievements as well as the Logos'), or else they are *not* our own achievements "at all" (in which case we have *not* actively participated in them). Does Cobb wish to claim that our achievements are only *apparently* ours because they are really God's achievements?

Cobb responds by stating that "there may be a real difference between us in our views of the relation of human to divine action. My understanding in Whiteheadian terms, is that the intitial aim, derived from God, opens up to us the possibility of acting freely and also directs us toward an optimum action. Hence, when we act, we enact some aspect of that which is given us as a particular possibility by God. This seems to me very close to the sense, widespread among Christians, that grace is prior to freedom. . . Rather than juxtaposing divine and human action such that the more God is active the less space there is for human action, I find it both Christian and Whiteheadian to affirm that the more God is active the more space there is for free human action. Our finest and freest achievements are the optimum enactments of what God's act gives us as real possibility."[199]

Most of Ogden's critique of Cobb focuses on the latter's attempt to argue for a distinctive structure of Jesus' existence that would parallel that distinctiveness attributed to him at Chalcedon.[200] The constitutive Christological assertion is that "Jesus is the Christ." But Cobb "entirely omits an analysis of the *question* to which this assertion functions as the answer . . . he offers a 'formal' definition of 'Christ' . . . he says " 'Christ' names what is experienced as supremely important when this is bound up with Jesus'."[201] From a parallel passage Cobb seems to indicate that "the divine reality" is "what is supremely important," and that being "bound up with

Jesus" means being "present and manifest in Jesus."[202] By implication, then, Cobb here identifies the question of Christ with the question of God, itself understood as the question of what is most important for human existence. But "he himself nowhere follows up this clue by explicating the existentialist analysis of the Christological question to which it points . . . his interpretation of the Christological assertion commits what one could properly call the fallacy of misplaced concreteness. Forgetting the existential context that, in the New Testament, at least, is the concrete context of this assertion, Cobb assumes that it has to do with the distinctive possibility of existence that Jesus perfectly *actualized*, not with the distinctive possibility of existence that Jesus decisively *represents*. And so he interprets it as an assertion about the *being* of Jesus *in himself* in abstraction from the question of the *meaning* of Jesus *for us*."[203] [italics added] If this is the case, then Cobb has completely abandoned the method of correlation — and, as we will see shortly, even the historical-critical approach to the central Christian affirmation regarding the Christ.

Cobb first undertakes to develop the "theoretical possibility" of a "distinctive structure of existence."[204] On this view, the Logos "is incarnate in all things," although "the mode and function of that incarnation vary."[205] This is particularly so with respect to its incarnation in human persons; for "there is little common human nature other than the uniquely human capacity to be shaped in history into a wide variety of structures of existence."[206] Having thus established its *theoretical* possibility, Cobb then proceeds to argue that this distinctive structure of existence was actually embodied in Jesus from the consensus of historians who have engaged in the quest of the historical Jesus that "at the heart of Jesus' message is an astonishing presumption of his own importance and authority."[207] Cobb's own argument here is a kind of reductive argument, i.e., from the alleged historical "datum" of "Jesus' implicit claim to authority" to his having embodied in fact the unique structure of existence that has been shown to be at least a possibility.[208]

Cobb's entire argument evidently takes for granted that we can know enough about "the real Jesus" to assert that he himself

claimed a unique authority for his personal word and implicity identified his actions as "directly expressive of God's purposes."[209]
The question is: how warranted is this assumption? Cobb seems
assured that "by working back to older layers of tradition we can
arrive at reliable information about Jesus."[210] But is it not more
accurate to say that no matter how far back we work through the
layers of tradition, the only thing given we can ever arrive at is itself
always only a layer of tradition? And even that layer of tradition,
will it not show every sign of being more concerned with bearing
faithful witness to Jesus rather than with giving reliable information about him? That Jesus' implicit claim to authority "is a more
or less probable *inference* from our sources, I, at least, am willing
to allow. But to speak of it as a *'datum'* seems to me to claim far
more than our sources warrant — and certainly more than Cobb
himself gives any reason for claiming."[211]

While Cobb again and again asserts that Jesus was the "fullest"
incarnation of the Logos, in that he embodied the unique structure
of existence in which all *tension* between the self and the Logos is
overcome, what he affirms or assumes as historically true of Jesus'
life in no way entitles him to make such an assertion. He writes
that "we may assume that the distinctive structure of Jesus' existence
did not characterize his infancy or remain constant through sleep-
ing and waking states. When it emerged and how steady it became
are subjects on which we have little information . . . (even if) the
stories of Jesus' temptation in the wilderness, his struggle in
Gethsemane, and his forsakenness on the cross are not historically
reliable, (they nevertheless) witness to the belief on the part of his
disciples that he was not continuously free from the tension between his 'I' and the Logos."[212]

Therefore, all that Cobb finally affirms as historically true is that
"at least at important times in his life Jesus freely chose to constitute his own selfhood as one with (the) presence of God within
him."[213] This now appears as a *highly qualified* affirmation. How
can Cobb write that and then feel entitled to assert that Jesus was
in fact the "fullest" incarnation of the Logos? By his own definition, the possibility of such a perfect incarnation requires that "the
'I' *in each moment*" be free from all tension with the Logos —

and this he not only does not affirm of Jesus' life but, by implication, denies of it. Notwithstanding, Cobb insists that the incarnation in Jesus was not simply an *intensification* of the presence of the Logos in all people; and he contends that Jesus would not constitute an image (symbol) of hope or creative transformation if he only participated more fully in the distinctive structure that we know in ourselves as Christians.[214]

Ogden even concludes that the method of Cobb's argumentation from the fact of Jesus' implied presumption of his own importance and authority leads to the conclusion that "if the fact of Jesus' claim to speak and to act for God could be explained otherwise than by his being the fullest incarnation of the Logos, then the most that Cobb could conclude is not that Jesus *was* that incarnation but only that he *might have been it* . . . the most that his argument entitles him to conclude is not that, 'so far as we know, Jesus *is* unique',[215] but only that, so far as we know, Jesus *might be* unique . . . by his (Cobb's) own account, any understanding of Christ must be grounded in the historical Jesus. . . . But this is just what such argument as he offers does not do at all and, significantly, does not even claim to do. For all Cobb succeeds in establishing, his christology describes a Jesus who is a mere possibility, not the actuality it purports to describe. Thus, it is at best a wholly speculative interpretation in no way grounded in the Jesus of history it professes to interpret."[216]

Cobb, of course, has his own critique of Ogden's observations. He assumes that "all beliefs about the past are hypotheses and in that sense merely hypothetical"[217] — so that he has not argued for any *categorical* conclusion. Hypotheses are on a continuum from well supported to poorly supported. Cobb contends that "the evaluation of my hypotheses should be according to where they stand on this continuum. If 'merely hypothetical' means 'not supported at all,' then I obviously do not agree, since I have gone to some trouble to support my theories"[218] — and he asserts that his hypotheses about Jesus have been relatively well supported. His hypothesis is not that Jesus' implicit claim "is a *true* or *valid* claim," as Ogden contends.[219] The issue for Cobb is not initially truth or validity but more generally how the occurrence of that implicit claim is best explained.

The question for Cobb is "whether the distinctive relation to God that seems to come to expression in Jesus' action and words is possible. If in fact God's relation to all persons is structurally identical, then the hypothesis arising from the effort to understand Jesus is undercut. But I have argued that there is a possible structure of existence that corresponds with the one that is called for by the historical interpretation. This allows the interpretation to stand. Such a procedure is speculative throughout and in no way *proves* the truth of the hypotheses, but I find Ogden's final conclusion much too strong. . . ."[220]

Cobb's hypothesis that in Jesus there appeared in an important way a structure of existence of whose occurrence elsewhere we have no evidence does not entail the improbable view (as alluded to by Ogden) that Jesus embodied this distinctive structure continuously from birth to death any more than Christians or Buddhists embody the distinctive Christian or Buddhist structures continuously. The structure of existence that appeared in Jesus is distinctive in the way in which God was constitutively present in important occasions of Jesus' experience. Cobb's hypothesis is that Jesus' prehension of God was co-constitutive of his selfhood with his prehension of his personal past. God is immanent or incarnate in all occasions whatsoever, but when God's immanence is co-constitutive of selfhood, we have a distinctive mode of incarnation.

Cobb insists, as opposed to Ogden, that he is disinclined to insist upon one point of Christology as *the* point of Christological exploration.[221] He feels that Ogden supposed that he thought that *the* crucial Christological claim had to do with the incarnation in Jesus of a distinctive structure of existence. In reality, Cobb only singled out this one point as the theme of his book. Cobb comments that he regards "the question about Jesus' distinctiveness as important in its interrelationship with other questions, but I do not assign it the centrality Ogden attributes to me. . . ."[222]

With Tillich, Cobb has proposed that we view the Christological question as changing from period to period — and today there is a complex of Christological questions. In **Christ in a Pluralistic Age** he has singled out (as of special importance) the question of the image or symbol of Christ as the Way of creative transformation. Cobb sees this creative transformation as existential, but also as communal, cultural, and world-historical. His discussion of Jesus, therefore, is designed chiefly to justify *this* Christological focus in relation to his work and person.

Cobb is somewhat akin to the thought of a fellow process thinker, Bernard E. Meland. He sees theology also as basically an instrument, not substantive in character, and, at best, something that can mitigate the mind's allegiance to despair. The Christian attitude is and ought to be one of trust, not certainty — a somewhat more humble stance.[223]

Cobb breaks some exciting new ground in his theological and Christological openness to other faiths, especially Buddhism. The two classic ultimates, Being/Brahman and the principle of rightness, are isolated. Buddhism dissolved Brahman into Emptiness, while a similar dissolution of Being has taken place at the hands of Heidegger and Whitehead (creativity). Instead of their identity, the two new ultimates, God and creativity, are both affirmed as incommensurable, and this is used as a means of appreciating positively the quest of Buddhism.[224]

While continuing to submit itself to creative transformation in its assimilation of new aspects of Western culture, Christianity needs to open itself to still more radical transformation through the Asian religions. The task is to be carried out individually with each of these great Ways, but the conversation with Buddhism is particularly urgent and fruitful. Whitehead did see that his philosophy of process had special cogeniality with some streams of Oriental thought. For example, with Buddhism it shares in the denial of substance, even though Buddhism draws conclusions from this denial that are religiously far removed from the Western Christian tradition. Another example would be the understanding of the human person. The usual Western view has been that there is an entitative self, or a subject of experience and action. The word "I" has referred ultimately to this transcendental or underlying self. But Whitehead and Buddhists alike deny the existence of this self. They both hold that a single human existence is only a strand of experiences in the total flux of experiences. The real entities are the individual experiences. The mode of connection that constitutes them as a single person is secondary to their individuality.

Buddhists know that *intellectual* acquiescence in this theory of the person does not necessarily entail *existential* realization of its truth. Human suffering is accountable for this failure of realization. Therefore, it has devised meditations through which the power of illusion can be broken and people can know who and what they are. To do this they must stop interpreting their experience and simply let their experience be what it is. What it is is *sunyata*, which is probably best translated as "emptiness." It is the coming together of what is not. To realize this is to be free from anxiety about one's supposed past or future or even present. There is no one about whom to worry.

At all times the real perspective is the internal one. From that internal perspective there is no series of coming-togethers; there is only the event. The unconscious supposition that we can stand outside the stream of events and observe them is false; the ultimate and true standpoint is always *within* the empty event of coming together. In that perspective there is no past and future; also, of course, no time. There is only happening.

Whitehead's account of the Kingdom of heaven or the Consequent Nature of God has remarkable affinities to this Buddhist doctrine of "emptiness." The ideal for the Buddhist is the nothingness or perfect emptiness. For Whitehead, the divine aim is at the realization of all possibilities "in due season" and therefore it interposes no particular principle of selection upon the Consequent Nature. Each element is allowed to be what it is. God is "empty" of "self" in so far as "self" is understood as an essence that can be preserved only by excluding "other" things, or at least not allowing them to be received just as they are. How would it affect our religious sensibilities if we thought of the Kingdom of heaven as the everlasting divine *sunyata* (or "peace")? Would this not support, by radicalizing, the Christian ideal of creative and responsive love?[225]

Cobb's analysis of the God-question vis-à-vis Buddhists is quite enlightening. He states that "the Buddhist is indifferent toward those features of our experience which led Whitehead to speak of God, i.e., purpose, accountability, qualitative novelty, order supportive of the emergence of intensities, and gradations of value. Thus Buddhists are not led by their experience to belief in Whitehead's God. But it would be too strong a statement to say that Buddhism necessarily denies the existence of God as Whitehead conceives deity . . . by (the term) 'God' it understands an ultimate ground of being, a substance underlying and relativizing the flux of events, or a static being transcending the flux.''[226] Consequently, the Buddhists often speak against belief in that *type* of "God." Process theology denies God in those meanings also. In place of an ultimate ground of being Whitehead speaks of creativity as ultimate. But creativity (in that sense), far from having eminent supratemporal reality, has no existence in itself and is to be found only in actual instances of the many becoming one. God in process is a formative element of the flux.

Since the questions to which God is the answer are not usual Buddhist questions, the God of process thought is not found in Buddhism; but divinities with somewhat analogous cosmological and religious functions do appear in Buddhist literature. Because of the possibility of discussing this processive God with Buddhists, process theologians should question how fully they have reflected on the meaning of the *non-substantial* character of God. Evidently, it is especially John Cobb who is doing this so that the encounter with Buddhism can lead to a creative transformation of process theology that will not deny its insights but will incorporate them into a larger whole.

These comments are illustrated in an exciting way by the poem entitled Buddha's "Pity":

My children,
The Enlightened One, because He saw Mankind drowning
    in the Great Sea of Birth, Death and Sorrow,
    and longed to save them,
For this He was moved to pity.
Because he saw the men of the world straying in false paths,
    and none to guide them,
For this He was moved to pity.

Because He saw that they lay wallowing in the mire
   of the Five Lusts, in dissolute abandonment,
For this He was moved to pity.

Because He saw them still fettered to their wealth, . . .
   not knowing how to cast them aside,
For this He was moved to pity.

Because He saw them doing evil with hand, heart, and
tongue,
   and many times receiving the bitter fruits of sin,
   yet ever yielding to their desires,
For this He was moved to pity.

Because He saw that though they longed for happiness,
   they made for themselves no karma of happiness;
   and though they hated pain, yet willingly made for
      themselves
   a karma of pain; and though they coveted the joys of
      Heaven,
   would not follow His commandments on earth,
For this He was moved to pity.

Because He saw them afraid of birth, old age and death,
   yet still pursuing the works that lead
   to birth, old age and death,
For this he was moved to pity.

Because He saw them consumed by the fires
   of pain and sorrow, yet knowing not where to seek
   the still waters of samadhi,
For this He was moved to pity.

Because He saw them living in an evil time, subjected to
   tyrannous kings and suffering many ills,
   yet heedlessly following after pleasure,
For this He was moved to pity.

Because he saw them living in a time of wars, killing, and
   wounding one another; and knew that for the riotous
      hatred
   hatred that had flourished in their hearts

they were doomed to pay an endless retribution,
For this He was moved to pity.

Because many born at the time of His incarnation had heard
Him preach the Holy Law, yet could not receive it,
For this He was moved to pity.

Because some had great riches that they could not bear
to give away,
For this He was moved to pity.

Because He saw the men of the world ploughing their fields,
sowing the seed, trafficking, huckstering, buying and
selling; and at the end winning nothing but bitterness,
For this He was moved to pity.

(LAO TZU, THE WAY OF LIFE by Tao Te Ching,
translated by Raymond B. Blackney, 1955, The New
American Library, Inc.)

The Christian is the one who confesses that the Christ as the Way
of creative transformation is the en-fleshed "pity" or compassion
of a nurturing God. The Christian God is frenetic, not static!

V. CRITIQUE and FIVE MAJOR THEMES

For the task of this thesis, my citations of all the authors has been quite selective. I have already critiqued in both a positive and negative manner the consistency or inconsistency of Pittenger and Cobb. My comparison of Tillich's "New Being" with Cobb's image of the Christ as creative transformation will revolve around five major themes!

Prior to an analysis of Tillich's "New Being," some preparatory remarks are in order. His "method of correlation" is extremely attractive to the sensibilities of modernity. However (as mentioned previously), Tillich's "answering" Christian theology presents Christian symbols in *ontological* terms. The particular responsibility of theology is, by using an *ontological* framework, to interpret the meaning of religious symbols or images. "God is the answer to the question implied in being."[227]

Tillich does his theologizing under the rubric that there is an existential relationship between the question of being and the question of finitude (including anxiety). As one studies the thought of Tillich, it is almost impossible not to have the impression that the philosopher-theologian must spend much more time on the topic of "being." He seems to be persuaded that "modern man had in his very gene structure, as it were, a dominant nominalist strain, a strong inclination to dissolve his world into 'things.' To correct this situation, for it was not exactly a healthy one as Tillich saw it, was not to return to the realist position of the Middle Ages with its claim to the validity of the universals."[228]

In his book entitled **Love, Power, and Justice,** Tillich specified his goal: "I want you to turn from the naive nominalism in which the modern world lives . . . to something older than both nominalism and realism: to the philosophy which asks the question of being before the split into universal essences and particular contents. . . . It is the philosophy which asks the question: What does it mean that something *is*?"[229] The issue of being and non-being is foundational. Tillich then resorts to what he calls "*ontological concepts*" in order to further the discussion; the first is the basic ontological structure of self and world — the subject-object structure; and the second is finitude, i.e., the "shock of non-being," the capacity to envisage "beingness" and "nothingness."[230]

For Tillich, philosophy and theology both ask the question of being. Ontology is his first and major philosophical interest. It has already been observed, too, in what high regard Tillich holds existential analysis and how for him theology and existential philosophy could aid one another in his methodological system. In brief, it is Tillich's thesis that human reason experiences a transition or "fall" from an *essential* to an *existential* state just as every other aspect of life does, i.e., it, too, needs "salvation." And the salvation of reason comes via the Christian revelation of the New Being in Jesus as the Christ.

My reaction to Tillich is certainly not as vehement as Kenneth Hamilton's stern criticism of Tillich's system-building when he remarked that "to see Tillich's system as a whole is to see that it is incompatible with the Christian gospel."[231] My uneasiness with Tillich is rooted in some of his abstract terminology. For example, it may very well be that Tillich has death in mind when he discusses that abstract "threat of non-being"; yet it is just as true that by the use of that phrase he denotes considerably more than just the terminal, physical act of death. He really speaks of a kind of dissolution that threatens all of life and the more general experience of all living beings dying bit by bit every moment of their lives.[232] It would be incorrect, therefore, to conclude in a facile manner that by "non-being" Tillich refers only to death.

Part of the difficulty, of course, is Tillich's dependence on *ontological* terms and categories. The point is: "this is a non-metaphysical age, and Paul Tillich may be guilty of a misjudgment in his effort to set up the existential question and offer the answer from revelation in ontological terms. Perhaps he is too classical, too much of a Platonist, to fit the modern mood. Does Tillich's definition, 'God is being-itself,' *really* strike at the heart of modern man? . . . modern technical man may well regard the ontological question to be utter folly, and any systematic expression of Christianity based on the concept of being to be *ipso facto* extremely suspect at best."[233] It does seem rather presumptuous to "mine" the universal dimension of human experience for its yield of God in ontological categories.

Some Scriptural theologians might be critical of Tillich's ontological emphasis due to the fact that for them Tillich's Christianity sounds like abstract principles as opposed to the personalism and concreteness of the Biblical witness. They might even charge that Tillich makes very little use of the Bible. Tillich's rejoinder to this accusation is that he has not constructed a theological system on a "historical-critical 'biblical theology'," but he asserts that "its influence is present in every part of the system."[234] And he contends that he does not ignore the directness of the Biblical symbols, but only that they always lead on to ontological categories. The whole of the Tillichian theology does seem to treat the Biblical symbols sensitively, seriously, and extensively. For example, his treatment of Jesus as the Christ who brings in the "New Being."

Yet, in another sense, Tillich has side-stepped an important contemporary problem in theology — the problem of Biblical hermeneutics. In his over-riding concern for ontology, it does appear that he has not struggled with the question of the relation between the meaning of the Biblical statements at the time they were written and the meaning of those statements for the twentieth century. He does seem to have a rather casual attitude toward the historical Jesus — and some interpreters have even accused him of supplanting the personal, direct intervention of God with an *impersonal principle*. It is even reported that Tillich once told a group of Japanese Buddhists that it was a matter of indifference to him as a Christian theologian whether or not Jesus lived![235]

There are then some critics of Paul Tillich's "Jesus as the Christ" and the concept of the "New Being."[236] In all probability the criticism made most frequently is that there is a hiatus between the historical Jesus and the universal meaning of the "New Being." That is understandable — because his position is really rather confusing upon an initial reading. On the one hand (as we mentioned), he does seem to brush aside any real need for the historical Jesus, at least for faith; on the other hand, he does assert that the concrete, actual life had to be present, or else existential estrangement would not have been overcome and the "New Being" would have remained only a quest.[237]

In all of Tillich's Christology one paramount fact stands out: his

In all of Tillich's Christology one paramount fact stands out: his striving to discover the universal dimension of things. Tillich regards the human person not in the particular but in the universal sense, i.e., the human person in his/her *essential* nature and in his/her *existential* estrangement.[238] For example, traditional Christianity has always explicated Peter's confession at Caesarea Philippi (Matt. 16:16; cf. also Mark 8:29, Luke 9:20) as the original witness to the fact that the person Jesus was recognized to be the Messiah of God. But Tillich begins his treatment of Jesus as the Christ by asserting that Christianity is what it is through the affirmation that Christ brings the New Being. He writes that "Christianity was born, not with the birth of the man who is called 'Jesus,' but in the moment in which one of his followers was driven to say to him, 'Thou art the Christ.' And Christianity will live as long as there are people who repeat this assertion. For the event on which Christianity is based has two sides: the fact which is called 'Jesus of Nazareth' and the reception of this fact by those who received him as the Christ. The first of those who received him as the Christ in the early tradition was named Simon Peter. This event is reported in a story in the center of the Gospel of Mark . . . and marks the turning point in the narrative. The moment of the disciples' acceptance of Jesus as the Christ is also the moment of his rejection by the powers of history. This gives the story its tremendous symbolic power. He who is the Christ has to die for his acceptance of the title 'Christ.' And those who continue to call him the Christ must assert the paradox that he who is supposed to overcome existential estrangement must participate in it and its self-destructive consequences. This is the central story of the Gospel."[239]

For Tillich, Jesus as the Christ is both an historical fact and a subject of faith, so that Christian faith must consider both aspects. He comments that "Christian theology as a whole is undercut if one of them is completely ignored. If theology ignores the fact to which the name of Jesus of Nazareth points, it ignores the basic Christian assertion that Essential God-Manhood has appeared within existence and subjected itself to the conditions of existence without being conquered by them. If there were no personal life in which existential estrangement had been overcome, the New Being would have remained a quest and an expectation and would not be a reality in time and space. . . . This is the reason that Christian theology must insist on the actual act to which the name Jesus of Nazareth refers. . . . Nevertheless, the other side, the believing reception of Jesus *as* the Christ, calls for equal emphasis. Without this reception the Christ would not have been the Christ, namely, the manifestation of the New Being in time and space. If Jesus had not impressed himself as the Christ on his disciples and through them upon all following generations, the man who is called Jesus of Nazareth would perhaps be remembered as a historically and religiously important person. . . . He could then have been a prophetic anticipation of the New Being itself. . . . The receptive side of the Christian event is as important as the factual side. And only their unity creates the event upon which Christianity is based."[240]

The heat of the debate over Tillich's system-building might have caused his critics to have overlooked something. It is true that Tillich knew that people had to live by faith alone. Tillich, however, still did approve of research about the historical Jesus.[241] But biblical criticism for him cannot even guarantee the name of Jesus in respect to the one who was called the Christ. Tillich states that "it must leave that to the incertitudes of historical knowledge. But faith does guarantee the factual *transformation of reality* in that personal life which the New Testament expresses in its *picture* of Jesus as the Christ"[242] (italics added). A "picture" does communicate reality, but it may not supply us with all the facts we would like to have. The historical Jesus we cannot know in accurate detail, but we can know the general "picture" or "image" of the man. Through the Biblical accounts a reliable "picture" or "image of him who was transparent to the ground of his being" comes through to us.[243] Tillich did want Jesus to be actual. It was important "that in *one* personal life essential manhood has appeared."[244]

Ferré, a critic who once said that a person had to be a Tillichian or a Christian, sees a clash between Tillich's ontology and his Christian theology, but still maintains that it is in the person of Jesus as the Christ that he attempted to bring the two together. Ferré writes: "And yet Tillich wanted Jesus to be actual not only as the key peg of his system, not only as the theological requirement of

Incarnation, but also for his larger thinking that pressed theology toward ontology, faith toward knowledge. Only if Jesus was actual could his life be representative and thus universally relevant."[245] According to Tillich, it must be remembered that faith was being grasped by ultimate concern, not acquiring sure and steadfast knowledge upon which a person then made his choice.

Langdon Gilkey has suggested that Paul Tillich is telling twentieth-century persons that God and language about him are not relevant within a safe, but narrow, circumscribed "religious" territory. God and "God-talk" are centered in a perception of the presence of the divine within the human. That which we call God is seen as real within secular institutions and experiences. Religious symbols, then, have validity as they address themselves to those critical questions that inevitably arise, sometimes quite unexpectedly, out of our mundane existence.[246] (Sounds very much like John Cobb?)

Tillich felt that he had unveiled the human nature which is not produced by culture but which is the presupposition of culture, i.e., the ontological question is not merely one of human nature but of the nature of culture as well. Finite persons in their state of estrangement are the creators of the structures of culture. People cannot escape culture. However, no culture can make people over into something other than finite. No culture can create non-anxious persons, and for that matter, when men and women cease to ask the ontological question or to distinguish between time and eternity, the finite and the infinite, they are dooming both the individual and the collective life of humankind. At base, the question of being was to Tillich a life-and-death question for humankind. In another perspective, sociologist Robert N. Bellah has expressed the same urgency by writing that "in order to break through the literal univocal interpretation of reality that our pseudoscientific secular culture espouses, it is necessary for religion to communicate non-ordinary reality that breaks into ordinary reality and exposes its pretensions. When ordinary reality turns into a nightmare, as it increasingly has in modern society, only some transcendental perspective offers any hope."[247] Theology does not exist in a vacuum — which is why Paul Tillich can be called a "theologian of culture."

Tillich contends that the quest for the New Being is universal because the human predicament and its ambiguous conquest are universal. The quest then appears in all religions where at times the New Being is sought above history and at times the New Being is sought in history (Judaism, Islam, Christianity). Tillich adds that in Christianity the decisive event occurs in the center of history, and that it is precisely this event that gives history a center.[248] Since the quest for the New Being is universal, likewise the history of the symbol "Messiah" shows that its origin transcends both Judaism and Christianity. Consequently, Tillich can state that "the universal quest for the New Being is a consequence of universal revelation. If it claims universality, Christianity implicitly maintains that the different forms in which the quest for the New Being has been made are fulfilled in Jesus as the Christ."[249]

Like John Cobb, therefore, Tillich was an ecumenist; and in 1960 he visited Japan and had many conversations with Christian ministers and missionaries and with Buddhist scholars and priests. After that, he confessed to "being somehow transformed through participation."[250] Later on he would reject the "comparative" method of the relationship between different religions, whereby one compares the concept of God, humanity, etc. Tillich proposed instead that the *telos* question be raised with regard to different religions, and in broad strokes he sketched two "telos-formulas" for his readers: "In Christianity the telos of every*one* and everything united in the Kingdom of God; in Buddhism the telos of every*thing* and everyone fulfilled in the Nirvana."[251]

In summary, L. Gordon Tait gives a concise, accurate description of "New Being": "Tillich began to sketch the picture of the Christ as the one who was the bearer of the New Being. He thought of the New Being as concretely as possible; it was the coming of the redemptive, creative power in actuality, in the Christ, the center of history. The moment of the coming is the *kairos*. The New Being, therefore, is the involvement of being itself in existence, which means that healing and creative power is operative, that the transforming action is continuous, and that the New Being itself is the essence of history. One of Tillich's leading insights for our time was the New Being, the new creation, the power of reconciliation and renewal which never destroys or replaces creation, but which renovates the old creation to make a new one, brought to reality through the Spirit who dynamically and creatively conquers life's ambiguities. As Christian theologian, Tillich's basic vision is that in the Biblical picture of Jesus as the Christ lies the depth of culture, and that New Being is the ultimate concern of every man and woman.''[252]

* * * * *

As mentioned earlier, we turn to our five major themes to attempt some coherence between Tillich and Cobb:

Theme #1: The new realism in religious inquiry that is shared by the neo-orthodox (Tillich) and process (Cobb) thinkers, stressing the radical otherness of God and the causal efficacy of this otherness over against the older liberalism with its idealism and mentalism. Process thinkers such as Cobb are really very patiently describing the workings of divine grace in human experience. The basis for their conceptuality is constructed upon the elaborate metaphysics of Whitehead. Cobb (and Pittenger too) stand unapologetically within the process tradition, all the while stressing the element of *empirical* realism within that tradition over against the rationalistic tendencies that process often displays.

They do stress the causal efficacy of the Judaeo-Christian legacy, indicating how it has shaped our culture down through the ages in ways too massive and too deep to be available for our conscious acceptance or rejection. We live more deeply than we can think. Presumably because the Church has focused upon the conscious acceptance of a communal belief, the new realism shared by neo-orthodox theologians, e.g., Tillich, wishes to strike deeper at its underlying roots within the culture — that historical matrix within which our faith decisions are made.

Both Tillich and Cobb could be classified as "theologians of culture," even though their metaphysical base for doing theology is quite diverse. The unthematized, at times, assumption of this kind of theology is that faith is to be understood not simply as a legacy of belief inherited from the past, but rather as a vital response to realities inhering within the immediacies of experience as a resource of grace and judgment.

The Judaeo-Christian *ethos* and *mythos* have been seminal and formative of Western culture. It has been pervasive, not just in dogmas, doctrines, art, and architecture, but even as the leitmotif of the whole of Western culture. The root metaphor for all this is that of the covenant relation between God and humankind; indeed, the redemptive theme is woven into the whole of Western culture. For this reason, the Bible is not just a primary document for the Church but a primal document for the *culture*.

The "new realism" in post-liberal theology as typified by Tillich and Cobb is at pains to point out the limitations of the human structure that make our language of the Other "fallible forms and symbols." The causal efficacy of this "Otherness" cannot be encapsulated within the human endeavor alone.[253] Bernard E. Meland's work illuminates the theology of John Cobb vis-á-vis Paul Tillich. Believing that the physical sciences were the leaders in the awareness that language is basically developing "disclosure models" rather than "picture models" (symbols), he thinks that philosophers and theologians have not taken sufficient cognizance of this fact. Faith is always more than words or propositions; it is energy — social, psychical, redemptive energy within individual human persons, within corporate action among groups, *with* the culture, expressing this grace and judgment of relationships (the covenant) in terms of the resources that heal and redeem the ways of humankind. This resonates with the "method of correlation" of Paul Tillich. Language may illuminate this reality, but it does not capture it nor do it justice. Theologians, therefore, should have a lively sensitivity to the dissonances of human existence, and to the less manageable Other than what we can conceptualize. This would render the theologian/philosopher wary of easy efforts to achieve philosophical precision in theological discourse.

Words are born out of a historical situation, and when they cohere with historical events they will be employed freely without thought of definition; but they can also fall into disuse when the culture does not evoke their usage; and, in the case of religious language, the words often remained in cult, e.g., ceremonials and confessions, when they were no longer at home in the culture. However, it might

108

be speculated, after Hiroshima and Nagasaki, words like "sin" and "redemption," "grace" and "judgment," "demonic forces" and the "Kingdom of God," "death" and "transfiguration" (and even "resurrection") took on a vitality and relevance that they had not had in three hundred years!

Since there are limitations on language, the theologian's problem is how to attend to that sheer event of *existing* (Tillich) which is deeper than consciousness very often, and certainly deeper than anyone's sensory awareness of it. Not everything can be comprehended in the analytical mode; it must be complemented by the *imaginative* mode or the "narrative vision." This does not need to imply that the raw event of "existing" is beyond human awareness or wonder or waiting. The process thinker will maintain very often that the "lure of certainty" has produced the idea of the Absolute Other, an idea that has become the goal for so much of Western thought — whether sought in the dogma of authority, biblical literalism, or human reason. But the notion of the Absolute can easily become a phantom of our conceptual world that has little to do with the concrete realities of lived experience.

Bernard Meland operates from two basic suppositions: 1) an acute awareness of the "marginality of intelligibility," and 2) a realization that our culture cannot extricate itself from the Judaeo-Christian *mythos*.[254] The new empirical method of realism advocated by Cobb and Tillich begins with the empirical witness in the present (to be found in the worship of the Church, lived experience, and the culture), moves on to the primal source and norm of the *mythos* (to be found in the word of Scripture), and then returns to the present demand for intelligibility in Christian faith. The segregation of the gospel from culture can lead to a theology of containment in which neither the full meaning of the Gospel nor the full meaning of the culture, nor, for that matter, the full meaning of the human person can be known or understood.

In a most attractive passage for our purposes, Meland sees the structure of Christian faith as "symphonic rather than logical. There is a logic implicit within its minor themes, but the overall movement of its affirmations presents a dissonant situation in which contraries are simultaneously acknowledged and disavowed . . . The resolution of faith is not a logical argument into which everything reasonably fits, but an arduous and long-suffering venture in negotiation in which conflicting claims, reasonable in their own right, are somehow adjudicated, or brought into a livable correlation without achieving full conformity or uniformity of meaning and purpose.''[255]

* * * * *

Theme #2: In Tillich's doctrine of atonement, the symbolic assertion that "God takes the suffering of the world upon himself"[256] could mean a literal participation of the divine in existential estrangement through the actualization of the Cross of Christ. Ewert H. Cousins has written that "the dynamic, sympathetic God of Christian revelation, who reveals himself as love in the person of Jesus Christ, is less at home in a world of static substances than in the dynamic, related, and novel world of process thought."[257] It should be remembered here that in our previous discussion we showed the congenial and almost parallel understanding of the *power* of the concept "symbol" in both Paul Tillich and process thinkers.

Does the statement of Tillich call for a symbolic or literal participation of the divine in existential estrangement through the symbol of the Cross? In this area, he seems to be somewhat ambiguous. Since Jesus as the Christ bears the New Being, there must be a conflict between this New Being and existential estrangement unto death itself. He writes that "only by taking suffering and death upon himself could Jesus be the Christ, because only in this way could he participate completely in existence and conquer every force of estrangement which tried to dissolve his unity with God . . . the picture of the New Being in Jesus as the Christ . . . is not the picture of a divine-human automaton without serious temptation, real struggle, or tragic involvement in the ambiguities of life. Instead of that, it is the picture of a personal life which is subjected to all the consequences of existential estrangement but wherein estrangement is conquered in himself and a permanent unity is kept with God. Into this unity he accepts the negativities of existence without removing them. This is done by transcending them in the power of his unity."[258]

The early Church had to defend the *factual* aspect of Jesus as the Christ, i.e., the Jesus character of the Christ and the Christ character of Jesus as the Christ. Arius attacked the Christ aspect; Nicaea defended the teaching that the power of Christ is the power of the Logos — as the Council asserted that Christ is of equal essence (*homoousios*) with God. Tillich comments that "the decision of Nicaea saved Christianity from a relapse to a cult of half-gods. It rejected interpretations of Jesus as the Christ which would have deprived him of his power to create the New Being."[259] It sounds here that Tillich might be asserting that the symbol of Christ as the New Being can only be predicated on the *literal* event of Jesus as the Christ. His comment infers that the decision of Nicaea substantiated that God himself and not a half-god is present in the man Jesus of Nazareth. Consequently, the loss of the Jesus character of Jesus as the Christ was averted, i.e., the denial of his full human nature.

Tillich, therefore, applauds the theological affirmations of both Nicaea and Chalcedon — and yet laments the inadequacy of their conceptual tools. The primary reason for this inadequacy lies in the fact that human concepts are incapable of expressing reality. According to Tillich, they are symbols. Therefore, the *homoousios* and the two-nature statements are inadequate. The two-nature statement does not fit for two reasons: 1) human "nature" is ambiguous and can thus refer to essential, existential, and the ambiguous unity of the essential and existential nature of the human person; and 2) God is simply above the term "nature." Such ancient classic terminology must be removed from current theology.

It is at this point that Tillich writes in terms that are quite reminiscent of a process/relational thinker. He states that "the assertion that Jesus as the Christ is the personal unity of a divine and a human nature must be replaced by the assertion that in Jesus as the Christ the eternal unity of God and man *has become* historical reality. In his being, the New Being is real, and the New Being is the re-established unity between God and man. We replace the inadequate concept 'divine nature' by the concepts 'eternal-God-man-unity' or 'Eternal God-manhood.' Such concepts replace a static essence by a *dynamic relation*. The *uniqueness* of this relation is in no way reduced by its dynamic character; but, by eliminating the concept of 'two natures,' which lie beside each other like blocks and whose unity cannot be understood at all, we are open to *relational* concepts which make understandable the dynamic picture of Jesus as the Christ."[260] (italics added)

For Tillich, Christology is a function of soteriology because it is the Christ who brings the New Being and thus saves humankind from existential estrangement. Christ's work is in the center of human history. He asserts that the sacred authors of the Gospels employ symbols to express the significance of Jesus as the Christ, as the bearer of the New Being. Tillich obviously does not reject this use of symbols (as mentioned earlier). On the contrary, he does not want at all a demythologization of the symbols, but rather a *deliteralization*.

Tillich goes on to consider what he calls the two central symbols of Christianity: the cross and resurrection of Christ. He comments that "the subjection of existence is expressed in the symbol of the 'Cross of the Christ'; the conquest of existence is expressed in the symbol of the 'Resurrection of the Christ' . . . (they are) interdependent symbols; they cannot be separated without losing their meaning. The Cross of the Christ is the Cross of the one who has conquered the death of existential estrangement. . . . They must be both *reality* and *symbol*. . . . One could say that in the minds of the disciples and of the writers of the New Testament the Cross is both an *event* and a *symbol*, and that the Resurrection is both a symbol and an event. Certainly, the Cross of Jesus is seen as an *event* that happened in time and space. But, as the Cross of the Jesus who is the Christ, it is a *symbol* and a part of a myth. It is the myth of the bearer of the new eon who suffers the death of a convict and slave under the powers of that old eon which he is to conquer. This Cross, whatever the historical circumstances may have been, is a *symbol based on a fact* . . . the only *factual* element in it having the immediate certainty of faith is the surrender of him who is called the Christ to the ultimate consequence of existence, namely, death under the conditions of estrangement. Everything else is a matter of historical probability, elaborated out of legendary interpretation.''[261] (italics added)

Tillich then finishes his treatment on *The Reality of the Christ* by offering a few words on the meaning of atonement. The Church has instinctively refused to state the doctrine of atonement in definite dogmatic terms; and this has opened the way for the development of different types of the doctrine of atonement. He comments that "the doctrine of atonement is the description of the effect of the New Being in Jesus as the Christ on those who are grasped by it in their state of estrangement . . . (it) is always both a divine act and a human reaction. . . . Atonement therefore necessarily has an objective and a subjective element.''[262] The Christ, as the bearer of the New Being, mediates the reconciling act of God to humankind.

In his fourth, fifth and sixth principles regarding the process of atonement, Tillich displays a remarkable affinity to process modes of thought — especially as regards the *literal* power of the symbol of the Cross. God's atoning activity must be understood as his *participation* in existential estrangement and its self-destructive consequences. God "can take them upon himself by participating in them and transforming them for those who participate in his participation. . . . The problem, of course, is: What does it mean that God takes the suffering of the world upon himself by participating in existential estrangement? The first answer is that it is a highly symbolic kind of speaking, but *a speaking which is not strange to the biblical writers.* God's 'patience,' God's 'repentance' (change of mind), God's 'toil with human sin,' 'God not sparing his Son,' and other expressions of this type disclose a freedom for *concreteness* in speaking of God's *living reactions* to the world of which *theology is naturally afraid.* If we try to say more than the symbolic assertion that 'God takes the suffering of the world upon himself,' we must add the statement that this suffering does not contradict God's eternal blessedness and its basis, namely, God's eternal 'aseity', his being by himself and therefore beyond freedom and destiny. On the other hand, we must refer to . . . the element of non-being which is eternally conquered in the divine life. This element of non-being, seen from *inside*, is the suffering that God takes upon himself by participating in existential estrangement or the state of unconquered negativity. Here the doctrine of the *living* God and the doctrine of the atonement coincide . . . in the Cross of Christ the divine participation in existential estrangement *becomes manifest* . . . Manifestations are *effective expressions*, not only communications. Something happens through a manifestation which has effects and consequences. The Cross of the Christ is a manifestation in this sense. It is a manifestation by being actualization. It is not the only actualization, but it is the central one, the criterion of all other manifestations of God's participation in the suffering of the world. The guilty conscience which looks at the Cross sees God's atoning act *in* it and *through* it, namely, his taking the destructive consequences of human guilt upon himself. . . . Neither is the suffering of the Christ a substitute for the suffering of man. But the suffering of God, universally and in the Christ, is the *power* which overcomes creaturely self-destruction by participation and *transformation.*"[263] (italics added)

Although Tillich does offer many qualifications in the atonement process — qualifications indebted to his existentialist ontology — the impression still remains that the symbol of the suffering God is rooted in the realistic and *literalistic* participation of the divine in the Cross of Christ. At least *implicitly* he does seem to attest that on the cross divine compassion absorbed humanity's worst existential depredations; and, in that mighty dynamic of love, the "God beyond God" accepts, forgives, and embraces humankind anyhow. To illustrate: a doctor, to treat a disease, has to expose himself to it! In a sense, although divine resources are considered limitless, the cross reveals that God, in his love and grant of free will to human beings, is somehow vulnerable to their perversity, swallowing up the grief, estrangement, and pangs of humankind's wrongdoing.

Suffering is not something to be regarded as negative — literally or symbolically. Therefore, for both Tillich and Cobb, the world's existential *hubris* and sorrow and agony are real to God. Suffering is capable of transmutation, and leads into deeper selfhood, community and healing. But this suffering does not only affect the community of humankind, because human peoples form a community not only among themselves but a covenant community with God.

It would seem that Tillich's "symbolic" assertion that "God takes the suffering of the world upon himself'' is much more heavily freighted than the conventional term "symbol" might suggest. His understanding of "symbol" is almost parallel to the process understanding of "symbol" where a symbol discloses a fuller reality than itself, and the basis for disclosure is that the symbol really *participates* in what it discloses. Tillich's analysis of the atoning process converges very nicely with the affirmation of Daniel Day Williams: "God does suffer as he participates in the ongoing life of the society of being. His sharing in the world's suffering is the supreme instance of knowing, accepting and transforming in love the suffering which arises in the world. I am affirming the doctrine of the divine sensitivity. Without it, I can make no sense of the being of God."[264]

* * * * *

Theme #3. In Tillich's conceptualization of the revelation of God in Christ, the man Jesus can only be seen as a transparent medium through which we become aware of the ultimate mystery of being that is transformative of human life. But also revealed (implicitly) is the experience which the disciples had in interchange with this man and with one another in the fellowship that formed around him and continued after his death. This is very congenial to process theological categories concerning the revelatory significance of the New Being. *Explicitly,* Tillich identifies revelation with the mystery of being; *implicitly,* he identified revelation also with the communion of discipleship which has the power to transform lives, save people from self-destruction, and bring them to the fullest actualization of the creative potentialities of human existence.

Before our analysis of the implications of the revelation of God in Christ in both Tillich and process thought, we must ask this question: Is it God's task to transform the world? According to Whitehead, "the consequent nature of God is his judgment on the world. He saves the world as it passes into the immediacy of his own life. It is the judgment of a tenderness which loses nothing that can be saved. It is also the judgment of a wisdom which uses what in the temporal world is mere wreakage."[265]

But does this mean that the world is transformed and the evil in it overcome, or only that it is included in the harmony of God's experience? Does this mean that the world is "saved" only by the method of conceptual harmonization in the experience of God rather than in an effective transformation of the world and over-coming its evil? Clearly the ancient Hebrew looked to Yahweh to bring about the prosperity of the Israelite nation. Some have argued that this expectation and hope was transformed by the proclamation of Jesus. For example, Samuel H. Beer writes that "the gospel of the kingdom is that there is another order beyond our earthly existence. Things of the world as we find it are mortal and so without consequence and meaning, except as they may be preserved in that saving order. Here the covenant with man is not that he and his children shall thrive and prosper in history. It is rather that they shall sooner or later die in history but that they shall yet live in an order which transcends history. The meek, the merciful, the pure in heart, shall inherit it, not on earth, but in heaven."[266] Consequently, are we to seek "a kindgom not of this world," a kingdom which both Beer and Whitehead find exemplified in the consequent nature of God?[267]

Whitehead would claim that what has already happened is past and cannot be altered; no future transformation can affect it. But it can be transformed in the divine experience of the world, and this is where its redemption is to be sought. Finite actualization is necessarily transient. He maintains therefore that "the ultimate evil in the temporal world . . . lies in the fact that the past fades, that time is a 'perpetual perishing'."[268] This "perishing" can only be overcome within a divine experience which savors every occasion, no matter how distantly past with respect to humankind's temporal history, i.e., as happening *now* in an everlasting immediacy which never fades. Whitehead comments that "each actuality in the temporal world has its reception into God's nature. The corresponding element in God's nature is not temporal activity, but is the transmutation of that temporal actuality into a living, ever-present fact."[269]

It might seem, at first glance, that the Kingdom proclaimed by Jesus has only a *futurist* eschatological dimension when translated into the process thought of Whitehead. Some would object that this ultimate consummation of all things is fine for God, but has no value for humankind. For example, George F. Thomas argues that Whitehead's God is not "the Redeemer of the world who transforms His creatures by the power of His grace and brings new life to them."[270] Sensitive to this Christian theological criticism, Whitehead develops his general "principle of relativity," whereby any actuality whatever causally influences all subsequent actualities, however negligibly.[271]

Whitehead speaks of "four creative phases" in which the universe accomplishes its actuality. The phases are:

1) God's originating activity in providing initial aims (grace?);
2) finite actualizations in the world;
3) God' complete experience of the world in his consequent nature; and
4) the impact of God's consequent experience upon the world.

Concerning this fourth phase, Whitehead comments that "the perfected actuality *passes back into* the temporal world, and *qualifies* this world so that each temporal actuality includes it as an *immediate* fact of relevant experience. For the kingdom of heaven is with us *today*."[272] (italics added). It sounds therefore like Whitehead does intuit the central motif of the proclamation of Jesus: that history is meant for Kingdom-building and creative transformation *now*!

These considerations should exonerate Whitehead and his process confreres from any accusation of "escapism" concerning the Christian God and the proclamation of the Kingdom. We return now to our theme of God's revelation in Jesus as the Christ.

According to Paul Tillich, the ultimate concern of the human person points to "being itself" which cannot be limited by any distinguishing characteristic whatsoever. As soon as you distinguish anything whatsoever you have a *kind of* being, i.e., *a* being alongside other beings. Tillich repeatedly denies that any such distinguishable being can be identified with God except by way of idolatry. To be sure, some distinguishable kind of being can be used as a *symbol* pointing to the unconditioned being that is beyond all characterization. But it is the unconditioned, which is to say "being itself" beyond all distinguishing characteristics whatsoever, that alone is of ultimate concern and that alone can be given the name of "God" when this word refers not to a symbol pointing on to God but to what is very God.

Against this background of Being Itself, Tillich does say some important things about the revelation of God in Christ. He maintains, first of all, that when we look for the revelation, the man Jesus as an actual, historical figure fades out (as mentioned earlier). What we find in place of the man Jesus is what Tillich calls the "picture" of the man represented in the New Testament — and this picture is not like a photograph, giving us a portrayal of the man as he was in actual existence.[273] The conclusion from this is rather obvious. It means that the writings of the New Testament depict the transforming power of the kind of interchange which occurred in the fellowship of Jesus. This is not what Tillich states *explicitly*, of course, but it does seem to be inevitably involved when he says that the New Testament is a "picture" which, like a work of art, interprets in depth the experience of the disciples in their fellowship with Jesus.

Secondly, Tillich does have some *explicit* statements concerning the revelation of God in Jesus as the Christ. When we look for the revelation we see not the man Jesus but the power of being for which and in which and by which he lived. Therefore, the revelation is not anything in the man nor in the fellowship but in the *transparency* of the man Jesus through which we see on beyond him and his life. Through this transparency we see not a loving Father (as tradition has asserted) but the awe-ful mystery of being. The suffering of Jesus, his rejection, his crucifixion, the apparent futility of all his striving, combined with his unwavering devotion (as pictured in the New Testament), obliterate the significance of the man except as a transparent medium through which we become aware of the mystery of being.

In other words, Tillich cuts through the vast problems of New Testament criticism and interpretation to make two telling points about Jesus as the Christ who is the final revelation, the one who actualizes "abstract principle in the concrete": 1) In spite of Jesus' participation in the ambiguities of human life, he maintains unity with God, the ground of all being. God's presence in him makes him the Christ. Tillich writes that "in all his utterances, words, deeds, and sufferings, he is transparent to that which he represents as the Christ, the divine mystery."[274] 2) He sacrifices everything he could have gained for himself from this unity. This is his victory over temptation. Jesus' unity with God could have been exploited as an advantage for himself — yet he resisted. During his life and at his life's end he accepted the cross. This is the acid test of his utter transparency to the ground of being. The final revelation, the revelatory event of Jesus as the Christ, takes place in a correlation of ecstasy and miracle.[275] Jesus as the Christ stands the double test of finality: unqualified unity with the ground of his being and the continuous sacrifice of himself. In this way Jesus reveals not himself, and not any distinguishable kind of being that might be called "God," but rather the mystery of the power of being. What is revealed is not anything knowable; what is revealed is the ultimate mystery.

Even though Tillich writes here in ontological terms, process thinkers such as Pittenger and Cobb could easily convert that conceptuality into expressions such as "God's initial aim" for Jesus and the "unique receptivity" of Jesus to that divine impulse. Furthermore, Tillich has really given two interpretations of that event which is called the revelation of God in Christ. According to the one *explicit* interpretation, there is the revelation of the mystery of being. According to the other *implicit* interpretation, there is also revealed the kind of interchange which transforms the lives of people in deep communion. Both are revealed. The question at issue here is this: which of these two revelations has the *power to transform* the lives of people to *save* them from self-destruction and bring them to the fullest actualization of the constructive potentialities of human existence *now*? It should be obvious that the process Christological thinker would opt for the latter implicit interpretation. The communion revealed in the fellowship of the disciples with Jesus is what has the power to do creative transformation. For the theologian of process the correct interpretation of the revelation of God in Christ is this creative interchange. It is felt that many theologians today agree *implicitly* that the communion which occurred in the fellowship of Jesus was and is the event necessarily involved in the revelation. But they fail to see that it *is* the very revelation itself.

*   *   *   *   *

Theme #4. In recent Whiteheadian process thought, the technical category of "proposition" has come into prominence. John Cobb's Christology in Christ in a Pluralistic Age has also appropriated this orientation. The God who acts in the world does so only through persuasion or lure, never through coercion. Only God "knows" the difference between embrace and throttle. The offering of an aim towards self-transcendence, towards greater intensity and satisfaction, towards greater stature of spirit, is explicated in Whitehead with the help of the category "proposition," especially non-conformal proposition. Whitehead has observed that it is more important for a proposition to be interesting than true. A non-conformal proposition is not now true, but *could* be. In its simplest formulation, propositions "are tales that might perhaps be told about particular actualities."[276]

The notion of "proposition" presupposes that human life is always open to growth and newness. The human person can always become more than he/she is at the moment; can always add new intensity to what he/she already is. When the person feels that there is a new possibility relevant to his/her life, he/she is experiencing a proposition, i.e., something is proposed or offered and he/she sees its relevance. For example, the sacraments of the Church can be categorized as "propositions" in process modes of thought. Each sacrament takes a form of definiteness (or a form of definition) that is in the Jesus-Event and proposes that form of definition to the Christian to become a form of definiteness in his/her life. A sacrament wants to make the Jesus-Event present by urging that some particular effects from the Jesus-Event be built into the structure of the Christian life. What a sacrament does in a ritual moment is to *propose* to the Christian that he/she accept certain components of the Jesus-Event into his/her life. Certain "ingredients" of the structure of the Jesus-Event are put into the structure of the Christian ritual life precisely so that the Christian can put them into the structure of his/her own being; so that some of the structure of that "New Being" can be built into the being of the Christian. Consequently, a proposition is that transaction in which a possibility is offered to an actual entity in an ongoing moment of experience for *possible* inclusion.

The category of "proposition" in process Christology would mean to speak of Jesus Christ as an enbodiment of a plan of salvation offered by God to humankind. And "because the notion of proposition is tense with contrast between past and future, it can carry a lot of eschatological freight. The loss of religious intensity can be attributed in part to the weakening of eschatological vision. The recovery of that vision is high on the theological agenda."[277] With Christian eschatology there is presumed a teleology. The becoming of the world has a thrust. The more *rationalistic* school of process theology would speak of a movement towards perfection or total harmony. The Christology of Paul in I Corinthians 15:25 works with such a vision. The *empirical* school of process theologians would stress rather a teleology of struggle towards greater stature of spirit (e.g., Bernard Loomer). This school gives the dissonances and ambiguities of life a metaphysical and not a provisional status. At the end of time in Matthew 25, there remain both good and evil in a final way.[278]

Our emphasis here is upon what Whitehead called "*non-conformal* propositions," i.e., a subject/predicate statement that does not conform to present fact, but suggests a possible future version of a fact with respect to some particular subject or subjects. The proposition is an entity that exists in the muddy waters between actuality and possibility. The predicate of a proposition indicates a possible configuration for a subject which differs from the present configuration. There is a contrast between what is and what might be, as in my previous example of the Christian sacraments. The contrast introduces an element of intensity into experience. Some intensity occurs even if the subject does not embark upon the new self or "new being." But sometimes the lure of propositions does move history.[279] In theological language here we could be speaking of the power that exists when one is under the claim of the eschaton. Intensity, power, and adventure are all involved here. Whitehead once wrote that "the death of religion comes with the repression of the high hope of adventure."[280] A familiar experience here to explicate the technical language would be what happens in our imagination when two alternative propositions are entertained. When the contrast between the present version of self and a possible new version of self is extremely interesting, it begins to compel not just attention, but also the energies requisite for its implementation. This is why Whitehead insists upon the importance of a proposition being very *interesting* if it is to get very far in promoting creative transformation.

God, therefore, has offered a "proposition" to the world about how it is to tell its tale in order to experience redemption. The objectification of that universal proposition in the Jesus-Event we name "the Christ." A corollary consideration here has to do with the word "world." Since the referent of that word is the web of relationality which has every actual entity in its embrace, a proposition to the world must mean that the tale to be told is primarily a tale about relationality. Transformation is precisely a re-creation of relationships. Christian "new being" (Tillich) is an emergent from *transfigured relationality*; and Jesus, as the Christ, is therefore God's "lure" to human history about "how to tell its tale" in order to experience creative transformation.

The statement that God offers the world a "proposition" in Jesus Christ must mean that Jesus receives from God a subjective aim that he embody a structure of relational existence to which every life is called. It must also mean that *other* human lives receive the subjective aim that they tell their tales according to the tale that is objectified in Jesus (although the life of Jesus is not the only disclosure of the plan of God). The point is that only individual subjects can entertain propositions. Therefore, a "proposition to the world" means an aim given Jesus in respect to future human lives, and an aim given future human lives in respect to Jesus.

Each of the propositions from God is grounded in what Whitehead calls the *primordial* nature of God, i.e., God's envisagement of the full range of the world's possibilities. The design of God, in which God's propositions are grounded, is single-minded. Every singular proposition of God reflects God's *universal* proposition. In Johannine terminology, the design of God is God's word, the Logos. We are reminded in the homily to the Hebrews that although the word of God has been spoken many times and in myriad ways, it is uttered with decisiveness in Jesus. (cf. Heb. 1:1-2) The words and work, the life, death, and resurrection of the Lord, all of these objectify God's proposition for the creative transformation of history. No *single* word or aspect of Jesus is the objectification of the proposition. The predicate of God's proposition is complex. As Lee comments: "The whole Jesus-Event is Christ-Event."[281]

The proposition which God makes to history in Jesus the Christ is a *universal* proposition. It is a way for all people to tell their tales. All human lives are the logical subjects of the proposition of God. The "tale," therefore, cannot be a particular form of human life. It cannot be tied to any specific cultural or historical configuration (as Cobb so brilliantly demonstrates). The proposition has to do with a structure of experiencing. Beardslee writes that "Christ does not stand for a predetermined form of human existence, but stands for a selfhood that is fully open to the momentary encounter with concrete beings which that existence encounters, in the faith that both such momentary but concrete encounters are of ultimate significance, and that the effort and hope, as well as the receptivity and 'realization' which such encounters embody, are not merely of the moment but are taken up into God's recognition and enjoyment of reality."[282]

John Cobb uses the expression "creative transformation" as the most generalized statement of the "tale" which the divine proposition, objectified in Jesus, presents. Cobb comments that "the Logos is threatening to any given world, for it functions to transcend and transform it. . . . In short, the function of the Logos is to introduce tension between what has been and what might be and continuously to challenge and upset the established order for the sake of the new. To name the Logos 'Christ' is to express and elicit trust. It is to promise that the unknown into which we are called is life rather than death . . . that is to say that to name the Logos 'Christ' is to recognize that the cosmic Logos is love. . . . It is a way in which the process of becoming is formed or structured. . . . To love in this sense is to constitute ourselves in each moment in relation to the future of others as well as to our own future."[283]

Cobb's use of "Christ" to refer to every objectification of the proposition of God for the world's creative transformation can be somewhat disconcerting. Although every proposition of God is grounded in the single-mindedness of the Logos, the word "Christ" is so deeply rooted in the Judaeo-Christian tradition that perhaps he should have reserved the title "Christ" for the objectification we encounter in Jesus.[284] It might have been better, therefore, had Cobb reserved the "Christ" title in this way — while standing with the very primitive Christian tradition which confessed the manifold presence of the *Logos*. For example, Clement of Alexandria defended philosophy as a manifestation of the Logos,[285] and included among those authentic, although partial, manifestations "the Indian gymnosophists, and other non-Greek philosophers, of whom there are two classes, the Sarmanae and the Brahamanas. . . Some too of the Indians who obey the precepts of Buddha."[286] There is also the rather startling witness of Augustine on this point: "The very thing which is called the Christian religion existed among the ancients, nor was it absent at the beginning of the human race, until the coming of Christ in the flesh when the true religion which already existed began to be called Christian. Therefore, if I have written: 'This is the true religion which exists in our days, the Christian religion,' the meaning is not that it had not existed previously, but that it took the name Christian only later."[287]

In summary, process Christology is saying that Jesus as the Christ is the objectification of the universal proposition which God has made to the world. The Church is the living, historical medium of God's offer because it is aware and is trying to make others aware of the contrast between what our lives are now and what they can yet become through fidelity to the Christ as "New Being" and as the image of creative transformation. "New Being" (Tillich) and Christ as "the symbol of creative transformation" (Cobb) are distinct *metaphysically* but *theologically* complementary in that both are attempting to explore this particular incarnation of God's proposition as a front line persuader of immediate experience to let the Christ-Event transform the world.

124

* * * * *

Theme #5. Which is more intolerable for Christian theology today: denying that God is a being, and so not being able to apply directly any predicates to God (Tillich), or making literal statements about God as a being, but not being able to distinguish absolutely God from all other actual being (process)?[288] The answer has astonishing Christological ramifications. It should be cautioned first that it is a perversion of the Christian faith to identify the revelation of God in Christ with any metaphysical system or with any ontology. This is true whether the system be naive supernaturalism, or Whitehead and Cobb, or Tillich. These systems come and go, depending on the prevailing form of culture and epoch in history. To tie Christian faith to any of them is to take our stand on a sinking ship. Deep communion in faith can go on regardless of the prevailing metaphysic. Each metaphysical system is a transitory perspective that an individual has attained. But creativity operates through history; new metaphysical systems will arise. Some of them may be more profound and comprehensive than any we have today. But none will be omniscient, none will be infallible; each one in time will be cast off by the creativity of history as it creates further visions reaching farther into the depths and heights of being.

Christian faith, therefore, must be commitment to this creativity and not to any one of the transitory visions that it brings forth in the minds of people. Life in Christ is life committed to the creativity that creates in each person an appreciative understanding of the vision of the other person and integrates these into a more comprehensive vision.

While it was always an error to identify faith in Christ with some metaphysical system or other, it was not a *fatal* error until now. Now we have reached a period in history when this false identification becomes suicidal for the Christian faith. The reason for this is cogently appreciated by John Cobb. It is simply this: we have come to a time of drastic pluralism when all the diverse cultures, systems, and people must live together in intimate association one with the other; when science is continuously revolutionizing our view of the world. Therefore, we must live in the power and keeping of the image of "Christ" as creative transformation. Cyprian Cooney has commented that "whereas Christian faith is a product of choice, Christian theology is a product of understanding. . . . As the subject of faith, Christ is a *constant*; as the subject of explanation, he is a *variable*."[289]

Despite all these precautionary remarks, we now make bold to propose a tentative and very schematic Christology for the 1980's that will weave together some Christological themes of Karl Rahner, John Cobb, Paul Tillich, Teilhard de Chardin, and W. Norman Pittenger. It is called the "anthropological-evolutionary model" of Christology. The representatives of this model want a 'unified' Christ; not God and man but God *as* man. They want to see Christ in terms of *creation* (Scotistic). Christ is the end, goal, culmination of creation. Hence, Christ is not explained "from above" but "from below" and "from within," that is, in terms of the creative process itself. In this way, Christ does not appear to be the exception but the supreme exemplification of the rule, or the supreme instance of what God is always doing everywhere in his creative activity. He is the focus (Pittenger). In order to overcome the dualism in Christ, which distinguishes and separates the divine and the human in Christ, an evolutionary model of thought is used. Living things are not matter plus life but living matter; humanity is not body plus soul but animated body. Jesus is not human plus God but divinized human. We have to see Christ in the context of creation and we have to see creation as evolutionary. God creates in an evolutionary way. God is the ultimate cause who through his causing gives being and enables a being to become and to transcend itself in becoming. God is always present to the evolutionary process and explains its movement from one stage to a higher stage. To the extent that God causes, to that extent, a being *is* and can transcend itself. Yet in the higher stage we do not have the former stage *plus* the higher stage as two distinct realities. The former stage is subsumed in a new way in the higher stage, which higher stage is a unity therefore and not a duality. As God causes, being becomes and moves to ever higher stages until we reach the human. At the level of humanity, moreover, something unique occurs. Humanity is matter that can turn back upon itself, that is, spirit. As spirit, the human is now a being whose very being is infinite openness, a *capax infiniti* (Rahner). There is no finite end to that which the human can become. No matter how much the human becomes, he/she remains human. The only "end" which humans can have as *capax infiniti* is the infinite or God.

However, and this is most important, all such becoming is due to the *initiative of God's causality*. Since the person is an *infinite* capacity to God's self-giving, to God's transcendental creative causality, God can give the *totality* of his *infinite* being to such a being. If God were to give his total being to a person, the person would not *cease* to be a person. The person would not move to a higher, distinct level of being and hence cease to be human, for the person is *open to infinitude* precisely *as human*. This fullest realization of the human, due to God's self-giving/causality, as well as the total acceptance of this divine self-gift is precisely what the man Jesus is: God's total self-gift, humankind's total acceptance of this gift. God has given himself totally to the man Jesus and Jesus has totally accepted this self-gift. Hence this human, while remaining human, is now *also* precisely as the *fully actualized human* (made possible *only* by God's creative self-giving) divine, but the divine of him is NOT SOMETHING DIFFERENT FROM THE MAN OF HIM. The divine of him is the perfection (or the perfecting) of the human of him. If a human being were to realize its infinite capacity (which it cannot do on its own, but only due to the creative causality of God), it would be divine, and this happened in Jesus. Jesus then is not man *and* God but God *as* man, or more exactly, divine as man. There is no division in him between human and divine. The divine is the human.

However, although with the above model we have unified Christ or proposed a *one nature* Christological model, the following must be noted:

1) It is not as if the human *ex sese* (in and of itself) were divine. The human only becomes the divine because it is fully actualized, and this full actualization is achieved *not in virtue of the human* but in virtue of the *divine self-giving*. Hence we can see that the divine of Jesus is always "gift" from God. Jesus' divinity is never *his*, something he "has" *on his own right*, but something given to

him precisely in virtue of the fact that the divine self-communicative causality perfects the human. In *this* sense then we must continue to speak of a distinction between the human of Jesus and the divine of Jesus. The divine does not "come from" the human as human.

2)   Although such a Christology gives us a unified Christology, a one nature Christology, this is not Apollinarianism or monophysitism. The divine and the human of Jesus do not so confuse as to eliminate the one or the other. Jesus never ceases to be human, nor does God cease to be God.

3)   In this model, Jesus, as the fullest actualized human, is himself seen to be the high point, goal and end of the evolutionary process itself which is constantly transcending itself (due to the divine causality) towards humanity. Once the human is reached on the evolutionary scale, one human (Jesus Christ) achieves the fullest actualization of the human, again due to the same divine self-giving causality. Hence Christ as both human and divine is seen to emerge from *within* creation itself. He is not a bolt out of the blue, for the same creative causality which is everywhere at work and makes possible creation in an evolutionary way is also at work in the man Jesus. Jesus, as goal of creation, is truly the *cosmic Christ* (Col. 1).

4)   With this model we have said all that Chalcedon demands: Jesus is truly one, truly human and truly divine. But this model does not make the divine and the human two "substances" or "natures" in Christ, in such a way that any true human history and growth on the part of Christ would be impeded. Edward Schillebeeckx puts it quite dramatically: "It is only in faith, from the life, death and resurrection of Jesus Christ that we learn that being man — the impossible — is nonetheless possible."[290]

5)   Is Christ, therefore, different from all other human beings in *kind* or in *degree*? Rahner himself is difficult to interpret when he poses this question to himself. Some statements seem to say that the difference is only one of degree, other statements seem to imply a difference in kind. However, several authors have noted that if Rahner is to be consistent with his premises and his metaphysical explanation of Christ, wherein he explains Christ in the context of creation (as its high point, goal and end), then Rahner should say

that the difference is one of degree and not kind. The difference between Christ and others is that he is not only *most* human, but *fully* human. Yet he is not human *plus* something else (distinct), namely, divine. We, on the other hand, never become fully human — the *capax infiniti* is never fully realized; it always remains *capax*, no matter what its degree of realization. However, we can also say that perhaps the difference of degree is so great, that in effect it amounts to a difference of kind (Cobb). We must also remember that Rahner's anthropological starting point (the human as *capax infiniti*) has itself challenged the Greek presupposition underlying the Chalcedonian two nature doctrine, namely, that there is between God and creature an infinite gap. For Rahner the human is not merely finite; he/she is a *relative infinitude*. Were this not the case, then how could the Word become flesh (Jn. 1:14)? He points out that Christology must not be dominated by the tyranny of a rigid metaphysics of infinity. Rather, metaphysics itself must be rethought in view of the incarnation.

In fact, while the classical tradition of Christology generally avoided using the language of "human person" in regard to Jesus, we can hardly avoid doing so today. Schoonenberg, for example, has observed that "human personhood, and thus an individual human being and becoming, and a human position in history, not only may not be excluded, but must be positively awarded to Jesus Christ."[291] Unless Jesus as the Christ truly belongs to our situation as an insider, and not as an outsider unaffected by the limitations and tribulations of our life (Tillich), he cannot meaningfully play the role of bringer of human salvation. The "text of his life is composed within the same context as our own."[292]

To be human is the gift of God. But the remarkable humanity of Jesus is due not only to God's gracious presence in him but also the creative responsiveness of Jesus to that gracious presence. He is the human open to God's gracious support, reliant upon it, trusting in it, responsive to it. We are unfamiliar in our experience with such qualities of singlemindedness, of unconditional dependence on the Father. These qualities stand out from us and apart from us, but they still belong to the realm of the human. They represent the human at its limit, in its *essential* character (Tillich), but they still represent the human. They represent the human as it ought to be, as it needs to be, as the possessor of "New Being." Thus, Jesus is like that luminously meaningful sentence we come upon in the middle of a book which lights up all the other sentences which have gone before and will follow after it; he is that uniquely special embodiment of God's Word which brings all other words to life with new meaning.[293]

* * * * *

Daniel Day Williams often focused on the theme of divine suffering. And Jung Young Lee went so far as to state that "the concept of divine suffering is not only the core of our faith but the uniqueness of Christianity."[294] Williams was an underestimated theologian due to the fact that he was normally identified as a process theologian. But "his theology and philosophical background is quite diverse and eclectic. In many ways he is a mediating theologian because of his willingness to draw insights from several traditions."[295] Williams' understanding of God reaches its logical conclusion in his affirmation of divine suffering, "a problem that somehow will not rest in the Christian mind and conscience."[296]

Daniel Day Williams was an expert on "God as love" and developed a Christology on those terms — relating it to suffering. He wrote that "in human terms, surely, to love *is* to be vulnerable — vulnerable to the hurts and risks that come from setting the other free and accepting his freedom."[297] Therefore, God suffers with Christ because "as Jesus suffers in his love with and for sinners, he discloses the suffering love of God."[298] He opposed the traditional view that suffering is inappropriate for God: "power is divine but pity is human."[299] Against the early theologians, Williams claimed that reference to divine suffering does not compromise God's deity, and atonement theories must reflect this. He commented that "Jesus' suffering has transforming power not merely as a demonstration of a truth but as an action which creates a new field of force in which forgiven men can be changed."[300]

Williams also asserted something about the other pole of God when he wrote that "the truth of impassibility [God viewed not as sufferer] is that God's love is the everlasting power and spirit of deity. . . . Unlimited love belongs to him as it belongs to no creature. God's love is absolute in its integrity forever. In this sense his love is invulnerable."[301] Yet God in Christ must suffer. Although God suffers, this does not imply weakness in God. For "suffering in the being of God is not just any suffering; it is the supreme instance of the transmutation of suffering."[302] Williams cites process philosophy, the Biblical theology movement, and the new concern for the atonement as the three most crucial factors in the "structural shift in the Christian mind" toward the affirmation of divine passibility.[303] If God in Christ does not suffer, then his love is so radically different from human love that it becomes unintelligible. If the Father does not suffer, Christ's suffering appears to be a price required of a callous God. God, therefore, suffers with us; he acts in the world to overcome our suffering; and he lures us to cooperate in the alleviation of suffering.[304]

* * * * *

A PRAYER TO THE GOD WHO FELL FROM HEAVEN

If you had stayed
tightfisted in the sky
and watched us thrash
with all the patience of a pipe smoker,
I would pray
like a golden bullet
aimed at your heart.
But the story says
you cried
and so heavy was the tear
you fell with it to earth
where like a baritone in a bar
it is never time to go home.
So you move among us
twisting every straight line
into Picasso,

stealing kisses from pinched lips,
holding our hand in the dark.
So now when I pray
I sit and turn my mind
like a television knob
til you are there
with your large, open hands
spreading my life before me
like a Sunday tablecloth
and pulling up a chair yourself
for by now
the secret is out.
You are home.[305]

*　*　*　*　*

"He who sits in the heavens *laughs*."
(Psalm 2:4)

BIBLIOGRAPHY

Anselm. **Proslogion.** M. J. Charlesworth, ed. Oxford: Clarendon Press, 1965.

Augustine. **The Retractions**

Bausch, William J. **Positioning: Belief in the Mid-Seventies.** Notre Dame: Fides Publishers, Inc., 1975

Beardslee, William A. **A House for Hope: A Study in Process and Biblical Thought.** Westminster Press, 1972.

Beer, Samuel H. **The City of Reason.** Cambridge: Harvard University Press, 1949.

Bellah, Robert N. **Beyond Belief.** New York: Harper and Row, 1970.

Bianchi, Eugene. "Holistic and Dynamic Development of Doctrinal Symbols," **Anglican Theological Review** 55 (1973).

Brueggemann, Walter. **The Bible Makes Sense.** Winona, Minnesota: St. Mary's College Press, 1977.

_____. "Covenant as a Subversive Paradigm," **The Christian Century** (Nov. 12, 1980.)

Burghardt, Walter J., S.J. **Sir, We Would Like to See Jesus: Homilies from a Hilltop.** Ramsey, N.J.: Paulist Press, 1982.

Cargas, Harry James and Bernard Lee. **Religious Experience and Process Theology.** Ramsey, N.J.: Paulist Press, 1976.

Carpenter, James C. "The Christology of John Cobb," **Process Studies,** Vol. 6, No. 2 (Summer, 1976).

Clement of Alexandria. **Stromateis**

Cobb, John B., Jr. "Buddhist Emptiness and the Christian God," **Journal of the American Academy of Religion,** 45/1 (March, 1977).

_____. **Christ in a Pluralistic Age.** Philadelphia: The Westminster Press, 1975.

_____. **A Christian Natural Theology.** Philadelphia: Westminster Press, 1965.

_____. "Response to Ogden and Carpenter," **Process Studies,** Vol. 6, No. 2 (Summer, 1976).

_____. "A Whiteheadian Christology," **Process Philosophy and Christian Thought.** ed. by Delwin Brown, Ralph E. James, Jr., and Gene Reeves. New York: The Bobbs-Merrill Company, 1971.

Cobb, John B., Jr. and David Ray Griffin. **Process Theology: An Introductory Exposition.** Philadelphia: The Westminster Press, 1976.

Cooney, Cyprian. **Understanding The New Theology.** Milwaukee: Bruce Publishing Company, 1969.

Copleston, Frederick, S. J. **A History of Western Philosophy: Vol. 1 Greece and Rome.** Westminster: The Newman Press, 1953.

Cousins, Ewert H. "Process Models in Culture, Philosophy, and Theology," **Process Theology.** New York: Newman Press, 1971.

Doud, Robert E. "Rahner's Christology: A Whiteheadian Critique," **Journal of Religion** 57/2 (April, 1977).

Dugan, Daniel O. **Faith for Tomorrow.** Dayton: Pflaum Press, 1969.

Dwyer, John C. **Son of Man & Son of God: A New Language for Faith.** New York: Paulist Press, 1983.

Ferré. Nels F. S. "The Fabric of Paul Tillich's Theology," **Scottish Journal of Theology,** Vol. 21, No. 2 (June, 1968).

_____. et al. **Paul Tillich: Retrospect and Future.** Nashville: Abingdon Press, 1966.

Ford, Lewis S. "Divine Persuasion and the Triumph of Good," **Philosophy of Religion: Contemporary Perspectives;** ed. by Norbert O. Schedler New York: Macmillan Publishing Co., Inc., 1974.

_____. **Horizons,** Vol. 4, No. 2 (Fall, 1977).

Fuller, Reginald. **Preaching the New Lectionary: The Word of God for the Church Today.** Collegeville: The Liturgical Press, 1971.

Gilkey, Langdon. **Naming the Whirlwind: The Renewal of God-Language.** Indianapolis: The Bobbs-Merrill Company, 1970.

Grant, Robert M. **The Early Christian Doctrine of God.** Charlottesville, Va.: University of Virginia Press, 1966.

Gray, Donald P. **Jesus: The Way to Freedom.** Winona: Saint Mary's Press, 1979.

Griffin, David Ray. "The Process Theology of Norman Pittenger: A Review Article," **Process Studies,** Vol. 6, No. 1 (Spring, 1976).

_____. **A Process Christology.** Philadelphia: Westminster Press, 1973.

Greeley, Andrew. **The Bottom Line Catechism for Contemporary Catholics.** Chicago: The Thomas More Press, 1982.

Guton, Colin. "The Knowledge of God According to Two Process Theologians: A Twentieth Century Gnosticism," **Religious Studies** 11 (1975).

Hamilton, Kenneth. **The System and the Gospel.** New York: The Macmillan Company, 1963.

Hammond, Guyton B. **The Power of Self-Transcendence.** St. Louis: The Bethany Press, 1966.

Hartshorne, Charles. **The Divine Relativity.** New Haven: Yale University Press, 1964.

_____. "The God of Religion and the God of Philosophy," **Talk of God: The Royal Institute of Philosophy Lectures,** 1967-68, Vol. II. London: Macmillan, 1969.

_____. Gordon D. Kaufman's **Systematic Theology: A Historicist Perspective.** New York: Charles Scribner's Sons, 1968.

_____. **Man's Vision of God and The Logic of Theism.** Hamden, Conn.: Archon Books, 1964.

_____. **A Natural Theology For Our Time.** LaSalle, Ill.: Open Court, 1967.

_____. "A Philosopher's Assessment of Christianity," Walter Leibrecht, ed., **Religion and Culture: Essays in Honor of Paul Tillich.** Freeport, N.Y.: Books for Libraries Press, 1972.

_____. "Process Philosophy As A Resource for Christian Thought," Perry LeFevre, ed., **Philosophical Resources for Christian Thought.** Nashville: Abingdon Press, 1968.

_____. **Reality As Social Process.** New York: Hafner Publishing Co., 1971.

Inbody, Tyron. "Paul Tillich and Process Theology," **Theological Studies,** Vol. 36, No. 3 (September, 1975).

James, Ralph E. **The Concrete God: A New Beginning for Theology — The Thought of Charles Hartshorne.** Indianapolis: Bobbs-Merrill Co., 1967.

King, Robert H. "The Task of Systematic Theology," **Christian Theology: An Introduction to its Traditions and Tasks.** ed. by Peter C. Hodgson and Robert H. King. Philadelphia: Fortress Press, 1982.

136

Kress, Robert. **A Rahner Handbook.** Atlanta: John Knox Press, 1982.

Kushner, Harold S. **When Bad Things Happen to Good People.** New York: Schoken Books, 1981.

Lane, Dermot A. **The Reality of Jesus.** New York: Paulist Press, 1975.

Lee, Bernard J. "The Sacrament of Creative Transformation," **Process Studies,** Vol. 8, No. 4 (Winter, 1978).

_____. **The Becoming of the Church: A Process Theology of the Structures of Christian Experience.** Ramsey, N.J.: Paulist Press, 1974.

Lee, Jung Young. **God Suffers For Us: A Systematic Inquiry into the Concept of Divine Passibility.** The Hague: Martinus Nijhoff, 1974.

May, Rollo. **The Courage to Create.** New York: W. W. Norton & Co., Inc., 1975.

McBrien, Richard P. **Catholicism,** Vol. I. Minneapolis: Winston Press, Inc., 1980.

_____. **Catholicism: Study Edition.** Minneapolis: Winston Press, 1981.

McWilliams, Warren. "Daniel Day Williams' Vulnerable and Invulnerable God," **Encounter** (Winter, 1982).

Meland, Bernard E. **Fallible Forms and Symbols: Discourses on Method in a Theology of Culture.** Philadelphia: Fortress Press, 1976.

Mellert, Robert B. **What is Process Theology?** Ramsey, N.J.: Paulist Press, 1975.

Niebuhr, H. Richard. **The Meaning of Revelation.** New York: Macmillan Paperbacks, 1960.

Nineham, Dennis. "God Incarnate: Why 'Myth'?" **The Myth/Truth of God Incarnate.** ed. by Durstan R. McDonald. Wolton, Conn.: Morehouse-Barlow Company, Inc., 1979.

O'Collins, Gerald, S. J. "Interpreting Jesus Today," **America** (October 1, 1983).

Ogden, Schubert M. **Christ Without Myth.** New York: Harper & Row, 1961.

_____. "Christology Reconsidered: John Cobb's 'Christ in

a Pluralistic Age'," **Process Studies,** Vol. 6, No. 2 (Summer, 1976).

_____. **The Point of Christology.** New York: Harper & Row, 1982.

_____. "The Point of Christology," **The Journal of Religion,** 55/4 (October, 1975).

O'Meara, Thomas F., O.P., and Donald M. Weisser, O.P., Eds. **Paul Tillich in Catholic Thought.** Garden City, N.Y.: Doubleday, 1969.

Osborne, Kenan B. **New Being: A Study on the Relationship Between Conditioned and Unconditioned Being According to Paul Tillich.** The Hague: Martinus Nijhoff, 1969.

Pannenberg, Wolfhart. **Jesus: God and Man.** Trans. by Lewis L. Wilkens and Duane A. Priebe. London: SCM Press, 1968.

Pittenger, W. Norman. **Catholic Faith in a Process Perspective.** Maryknoll N.Y.: Orbis Books, 1981.

_____. **Christology Reconsidered.** London: SCM Press. 1970.

_____. **The Lure of Divine Love.** Pilgrim Press, 1979.

_____. "Meland, Process Thought and Significance of Christ." **Process Theology.** ed. by Ewert H. Cousins. New York: Newman Press, 1971.

_____. **The Word Incarnate.** New York: Harper, 1959.

Prusak, Bernard P. "Changing Concepts of God and Their Repercussions in Christology." **Does Jesus Make a Difference?** ed. by Thomas M. McFadden. New York: The Seabury Press, 1974.

Rahner, Karl. "On the Theology of the Incarnation," **Theological Investigations, Vol. IV: More Recent Writings.** Baltimore: Helicon Press, 1966.

_____ and Herbert Vorgrimler. **Dictionary of Theology.** 2nd ed. New York: Crossroad Publishing Company, 1981.

Robinson, James M. **A New Quest of the Historical Jesus.** London: SCM Press, 1963.

Robinson, John A. T. **Honest to God.** Philadelphia: Westminster Press, 1963.

_____. **The Human Face of God.** Philadelphia: Westminster Press, 1973.

Schillebeeckx, Edward. **God: The Future of Man.** New York: Sheed and Ward, 1968.

Schilling, S. Paul. **God Incognito.** Nashville: Abingdon Press, 1974.

Schoonenberg, Piet. **The Christ.** New York: Seabury Press, 1971.

Shea, John. **Stories of God: An Unauthorized Biography.** Chicago: The Thomas More Press, 1978.

_____. **The God Who Fell From Heaven.** Niles, Ill.: Argus Communications, 1979.

Sloyan, Gerard S. **Jesus in Focus: A Life in its Setting.** Mystic, Conn.: Twenty-Third Publications, 1983.

Sykes, Stephen. **An Introduction to Christian Theology Today.** Atlanta: John Knox Press, 1974.

Tait, L. Gordon. **The Promise of Tillich.** Philadelphia: J. B. Lippincott Company, 1971.

Tavard, George H. **Paul Tillich and the Christian Message.** New York: Charles Scribner's Sons, 1962.

Thomas, George F. **Religious Philosophies of The West.** New York: Charles Scribner's Sons, 1965.

Thomas, J. Heywood. **Paul Tillich: An Appraisal.** Philadelphia: The Westminster Press, 1963.

Tillich, Paul. **Biblical Religion and the Search for Ultimate Reality.** Chicago: University of Chicago Press, 1955.

_____. **Christianity and the Encounter of the World Religions.** New York: Columbia University Press, 1963.

_____. **Dynamics of Faith.** New York: Harper and Row, 1957.

_____. **Love, Power, and Justice.** New York: Oxford University Press, 1954.

_____. "On the Boundary Line," **The Christian Century,** Vol. LXXVII, No. 49 (December 7, 1960).

_____. **Systematic Theology.** Vol. I. Chicago: The University of Chicago Press, 1951.

_____. **Systematic Theology.** Vol. II. Chicago: The University of Chicago Press, 1957.

_____. **The Protestant Era.** Chicago: The University of Chicago Press, 1948.

_____. **The Shaking of the Foundations.** New York: Charles Scribner's Sons, 1948.

Tracy, David. **Blessed Rage for Order: The New Pluralism in Theology.** New York: Seabury Press, 1978.

_____ and John B. Cobb, Jr. **Talking about God: Doing Theology in the Context of Modern Pluralism.** New York: Seabury Press, 1983.

Whitehead, Alfred North. **Process and Reality: An Essay in Cosmology.** New York: Macmillan, 1929, 6th rpt., 1967.

_____. **Religion in the Making.** Cleveland: Meridian Books, 1965.

_____. **Science and the Modern World.** New York: The Macmillan Company, 1925.

Williams, Daniel Day. "Suffering and Being in Empirical Theology," **The Future of Empirical Theology.** Bernard E. Meland, ed. Chicago: University of Chicago Press, 1969.

_____. **The Spirit and the Forms of Love.** New York: Harper & Row, 1968.

_____. "The Vulnerable and the Invulnerable God," **Christianity and Crisis,** Vol. 22 (March 5, 1962).

_____. **What Present Day Theologians are Thinking.** 3rd ed. New York: Harper & Row, 1967.

Williams, Ronald L. "The Two Types of Christology: A Neoclassical Analysis," **Journal of Religion** 49 (1969).

NOTES

[1] Walter Brueggemann, **The Bible Makes Sense** (Winona, Minnesota: St. Mary's College Press, 1977), pp. 99-100.

[2] Andrew Greeley, **The Bottom Line Catechism for Contemporary Catholics** (Chicago: The Thomas More Press, 1982), pp. 18-20.

[3] Frederick Copleston, S.J., **A History of Western Philosophy: Vol. I - Greece and Rome** (Westminster: The Newman Press, 1953), p. 317.

[4] Daniel O. Dugan, **Faith for Tomorrow** (Dayton: Pflaum Press, 1969), pp. 144-45.

[5] cf. Stephen Sykes, **An Introduction to Christian Theology Today** (Atlanta: John Knox Press, 1974), p. 18.

[6] cf. Robert M. Grant, **The Early Christian Doctrine of God** (Charlottesville, Va.: University of Virginia Press, 1966), pp. 4-5.

[7] Anselm, **Proslogian,** Chapter 8, M.J. Charlesworth, ed. (Oxford: Clarendon Press, 1965), pp. 124-25.

[8] Harold S. Kushner, **When Bad Things Happen to Good People** (New York: Schocken Books, 1981), p.42.

[9] cf. Reginald Fuller, **Preaching the New Lectionary: The Word of God for the Church Today** (Collegeville: The Liturgical Press, 1971), p. 104.

[10] Richard P. McBrien, **Catholicism,** Vol. I (Minneapolis: Winston Press, Inc., 1980), pp. 119-120.

[11] William J. Bausch, **Positioning: Belief in the Mid-Seventies** (Notre Dame: Fides Publishers, Inc., 1975), p. 36.

[12] Bernard P. Prusak, "Changing Concepts of God and Their Repercussions in Christology," **Does Jesus Make a Difference?** , ed. by Thomas M. McFadden (New York: The Seabury Press, 1974), p. 69.

[13] Karl Rahner, "On the Theology of the Incarnation," in **Theological Investigations, Vol. IV: More Recent Writings** (Baltimore: Helicon Press, 1966), p. 112.

[14] **Ibid.**, p. 113.

[15] Robert Kress, **A Rahner Handbook** (Atlanta: John Knox Press, 1982), p. 82.

142

[16] Alfred North Whitehead, **Religion in the Making** (New York: The World Publishing Company, 1967), p. 81.

[17] Robert H. King, "The Task of Systematic Theology," in **Christian Theology: An Introduction to its Traditions and Tasks,** ed. by Peter C. Hodgson and Robert H. King (Philadelphia: Fortress Press, 1982), pp. 22-23.

[18] Dennis Nineham, "God Incarnate: Why 'Myth'?" in **The Myth/Truth of God Incarnate,** ed. by Durstan R. McDonald (Wilton, Conn.: Morehouse-Barlow Co., Inc., 1979), pp. 65-66.

[19] cf. Alfred North Whitehead, **Process and Reality: An Essay in Cosmology** (New York: Macmillan, 1929, 6th rept., 1967), p. 520.

[20] **Ibid.**, p. 521.

[21] **Ibid.**, p. 522.

[22] **Ibid.**, p. 524.

[23] **Ibid.**, p. 528.

[24] **Ibid.**, pp. 27-28, 53, 101-04, 320-23, and 530.

[25] **Ibid.**, p. 528.

[26] **Ibid.**, pp. 522, 129-31, 46-48, 104, 248, 342-43.

[27] **Ibid.**, p. 527.

[28] **Ibid.**, p. 529.

[29] Charles Hartshorne, **Man's Vision of God and the Logic of Theism** (Hamden, Conn.: Archon Books, 1964), pp. 22-23.

[30] **Ibid.**, pp. 50-51 and 230-50.

[31] Whitehead, **op.cit.**, p. 532.

[32] Prusak, **op.cit.**, p. 73.

[33] Whitehead, **op.cit.**, p. 527.

[34] Hartshorne, **op.cit.**, p. 348.

[35] Charles Hartshorne, as quoted in Gordon D. Kaufman, **Systematic Theology: A Historicist Perspective** (New York: Charles Scribner's Sons, 1968), p. 213.

[36] Karl Rahner and Herbert Vorgrimler, **Dictionary of Theology**, 2nd ed., (New York: Crossroad Publishing Co., 1981), pp. 359-60.

[37] Prusak, **op.cit.**, p. 73.

[38] David Tracy, **Blessed Rage for Order: The New Pluralism in Theology** (New York: Seabury Press, 1975), p. 172.

[39] **Ibid.**, p. 174.

[40] cf. Piet Schoonenberg, **The Christ** (New York: Seabury Press, 1971).

[41] Dermot A. Lane, **The Reality of Jesus** (New York: Paulist Press, 1975), p. 118.

[42] W. Norman Pittenger, "Meland, Process Thought and Significance of Christ," in **Process Theology**, ed. by Ewert H. Cousins (New York: Newman Press, 1971), pp. 205-06.

[43] Walter J. Burghardt, S.J., **Sir, We Would Like to See Jesus: Homilies from a Hilltop** (Ramsey, N.J.: Paulist Press, 1982), pp. 106-108.

[44] John Shea, **Stories of God: An Unauthorized Biography** (Chicago: The Thomas More Press, 1978), p. 170.

[45] Walter Brueggeman, "Covenant as a Subversive Paradigm," in **The Christian Century** (Nov. 12, 1980), pp. 1094-1099.

[46] Rollo May, **The Courage to Create** (New York: W. W. Norton & Company, Inc., 1975), p. 44.

[47] Charles Hartshorne, **The Divine Relativity** (New Haven: Yale University Press, 1964), p. 50.

[48] cf. Ralph E. James. **The Concrete God** (Indianapolis: Bobbs-Merrill Co., Inc., 1967), p. 49.

[49] Charles Hartshorne, **A Natural Theology For Our Time** (LaSalle, Ill.: Open Court, 1967), p. 26.

[50] **Ibid.**, p. 75.

[51] Hartshorne, "Process Philosophy As a Resource for Christian Thought," in Perry LeFevre, ed., **Philosophical Resources for Christian Thought** (Nashville: Abingdon Press, 1968), p. 65.

[52] Charles Hartshorne, **Reality as Social Process** (New York: Hafner Publishing Co., 1971), p. 196.

[53] Charles Hartshorne, "The God of Religion and the God of Philosophy," in **Talk of God:** The Royal Institute of Philosophy Lectures, 1967-68, Vol. II (London: Macmillan, 1969), p. 159.

[54] cf. Hartshorne, **The Divine Relativity**, p. 54.

[55] cf. Charles Hartshorne, **Man's Vision of God** (Hamden, Conn.: Archon Books, 1964), pp. xvii-xix.

[56] **Ibid.**, p. viii.

[57] Hartshorne, "Process Philosophy As A Resource For Christian Thought," p. 63.

[58] Charles Hartshorne, "A Philosopher's Assessment of Christianity," in Walter Liebrecht, ed., **Religion and Culture: Essays in Honor of Paul Tillich** (Freeport, N.Y.: Books for Libraries Press, 1972), p. 180.

[59] **Ibid.,** p. 175.

[60] cf. Ralph James. **The Concrete God,** pp. 130ff.

[61] cf. Ronald L. Williams, "The Two Types of Christology: A Neoclassical Analysis," **Journal of Religion** 49 (1969), pp. 18-40. Williams maintains that the idea of 'Christology' itself is derivative from a conception of God and can, therefore, be separated from the church's historical Christology.

[62] Hartshorne, "The God of Religion and the God of Philosophy," p. 155.

[63] cf. Hartshorne, **Man's Vision of God and The Logic of Theism** (Hamden, Co.: Archon Books, 1964), pp. 174-211.

[64] cf. Colin Gunton, "The Knowledge of God According to Two Process Theologians: A Twentieth Century Gnosticism," **Religious Studies** 11 (1975), pp. 87-96.

[65] Alfred North Whitehead, **Religion in the Making** (Cleveland: Meridian Books, 1965), p. 148; cf. also Hartshorne's lengthy development of this theme in **Man's Vision of God,** pp. 174-211; also **Reality as Social Process,** pp. 141-142.

[66] cf. Hartshorne, **The Divine Relativity,** pp. 37ff.

[67] cf. Hartshorne, **Reality As Social Process,** pp. 147-149.

[68] **Ibid.,** p. 150.

[69] **Ibid.,** pp. 152-153.

[70] **Ibid.,** p. 153.

[71] cf. Wolfhart Pannenberg, **Jesus: God And Man,** trans. by Lewis L. Wilkens and Duane A. Priebe (London: SCM Press, 1968), pp. 158-168.

[72] cf. Ralph James. **The Concrete God** (Indianapolis: Bobbs-Merrill Co., Inc., 1967), pp. 149-169.

[73] **Ibid.,** p. 152.

[74] **Ibid.,** p. 168.

[75] Eugene Bianchi, "Holistic and Dynamic Development of Doctrinal Symbols," in **American Theological Review** 55 (1973), p. 158.

[76] cf. W. Norman Pittenger, **Christology Reconsidered** (London: SCM Press, 1970), pp. 19ff; pp. 109ff.; pp. 124ff.

[77] **Ibid.**, pp. 30-31.

[78] **Ibid.**, p. 98; cf. also p. 99.

[79] **Ibid.** , p. 68; cf. also p. 67, p. 78.

[80] **Ibid.**, p. 145.

[81] **Ibid.**, pp. 145-146.

[82] **Ibid.**, p. 73.

[83] **Ibid.**, p. 145.

[84] David Ray Griffin, "The Process Theology of Norman Pittenger: A Review Article," in **Process Studies**, Vol. 6, No. 1 (Spring 1976), p. 139.

[85] cf. Pittenger, **Christology Reconsidered**, p. 96.

[86] **Ibid.**, pp. 3; 86.

[87] **Ibid.**, p. 11.

[88] **Ibid.**, p. 151.

[89] **Ibid.**, pp. 139, 150, 102.

[90] **Ibid.**, pp. 112, 120, 124, 143.

[91] **Ibid.**, pp. 97, 152.

[92] **Ibid.**, pp. 50, 52, 54, 59, 60, 139, 143.

[93] **Ibid.**, p. 113.

[94] Pittenger, **Christology Reconsidered**, p. 58.

[95] **Ibid.**, p. 114.

[96] **Ibid.**, pp. 142ff.

[97] **Ibid.**, p. 143.

[98] cf. David Ray Griffin, **op.cit.**, p. 141.

[99] cf. Pittenger, **Christology Reconsidered**, pp. 89-93.

[100] **Ibid.**, pp. 126-128.

[101] David Ray Griffin, **op.cit.** in **"Process Studies,"** p. 144.

[102] Richard McBrien, **Catholicism: Study Edition** (Minneapolis: Winston Press, 1981), pp. 490-91; cf. also Norman Pittenger, **Christology Reconsidered** (London: SCM Press, 1970).

[103] cf. James M. Robinson, **A New Quest of the Historical Jesus** (London: SCM Press, 1963).

[104] John B. Cobb, Jr., "A Whiteheadian Christology," in **Process Philosophy and Christian Thought**, ed. by Delwin Brown, Ralph E. James, Jr., Gene Reeves (Indianapolis: Bobbs-Merrill, 1971), pp. 382-383.

[105] cf. Bernard Lee, S.M., **The Becoming of The Church: A Process Theology of the Structures of Christian Experience** (New York: Paulist Press, 1974), pp. 114-115.

[106] cf. Cobb. "A Whiteheadian Christology," in **Process Philosophy and Christian Thought**, ed. by Delwin Brown, Ralph E. James, and Gene Reeves (New York: The Bobbs-Merrill Company, 1971), pp. 383-385.

[107] James C. Carpenter, "The Christology of John Cobb," in **Process Studies**, Vol. 6, No. 2 (Summer, 1976), p. 103.

[108] cf. John B. Cobb. Jr., **A Christian Natural Theology** (Philadelphia: The Westminster Press, 1965), pp. 188, 192.

[109] **Ibid.**, pp. 176ff.

[110] John B. Cobb, Jr., "Response to Ogden and Carpenter," in **Process Studies**, Vol. 6, No. 2 (Summer, 1976), p. 127.

[111] **Ibid.**, p. 127.

[112] cf. Lee, **op.cit.**, p. 117.

[113] John B. Cobb. Jr., "A Whiteheadian Christology," **op.cit.**, pp. 390-393, passim.

[114] Lee, **op.cit.**, p. 199.

[115] John C. Dwyer, **Son of Man & Son of God: A New Language for Faith** (New York: Paulist Press, 1983), p. 33.

[116] **Ibid.**, p. 40.

[117] Gerard S. Sloyan, **Jesus in Focus: A Life in its Setting** (Mystic, Conn.: Twenty-Third Publications, 1983), p. 186.

[118] Lee, **op.cit.**, p. 201.

[119] **Ibid.**, pp. 204-05.

[120] **Ibid.**, pp. 205-06.

[121] cf. Lee, **Ibid.**, p. 206-07.

[122] John Cobb, "A Whiteheadian Christology," in **Process Philosophy and Christian Thought**, ed. by Delwin Brown, Ralph E. James, Jr., and Gene Reeves (New York: The Bobbs-Merrill Company, 1971), pp. 397-98.

[123] cf. James Carpenter, "The Christology of John Cobb," In **Process Studies**, Vol. 6, No. 2 (Summer, 1976), pp. 108-09.

[124] **Ibid.**, p. 109.

[125] **Ibid.**, pp. 110-11.

[126] cf. John B. Cobb., Jr., "Response to Ogden and Carpenter," in **Process Studies**, Vol. 6, No. 2 (Summer, 1976), p. 128.

[127] Cobb, "Response to Ogden and Carpenter," p. 128.

[128] **Ibid.**, p. 128.

[129] John B. Cobb, Jr., **A Christian Natural Theology** (Philadelphia: Westminster Press, 1965), pp. 180ff.

[130] **Ibid.**, pp. 226ff.

[131] **Ibid.**, pp. 227, 251.

[132] cf. Cobb. "A Whiteheadian Christology," **op.cit.**, p. 388.

[133] **Ibid.**, p. 398.

[134] cf. James Carpenter, **op.cit.** p. 112.

[135] John B. Cobb, Jr., "Response to Ogden and Carpenter," **op.cit.** p. 129.

[136] **Ibid.**, p. 129.

[137] John B. Cobb, Jr., **Christ in a Pluralistic Age** (Philadelphia: The Westminster Press, 1975).

[138] **Ibid.**, p. 21.

[139] **Ibid.**, pp. 21-22.

[140] Paul Tillich, **Systematic Theology**, Vol. 1 (Chicago: The University of Chicago Press, 1951), p. 49.

[141] John B. Cobb. Jr., **Christ in a Pluralistic Age**, p. 22.

[142] cf. Paul Tillich, **Dynamics of Faith** (New York: Harper & Row, Publishers, 1957), pp. 11-12.

[143] Paul Tillich, **The Shaking of the Foundations** (New York: Charles Scribner's Sons, 1948), p. 42.

[144] Paul Tillich, **Systematic Theology**, Vol. I., (Chicago: The University of Chicago Press, 1951), p. 12.

[145] cf. S. Paul Schilling, **God Incognito** (Nashville: Abingdon Press 1974), pp. 119-20.

[146] Paul Tillich, **The Protestant Era** (Chicago: University of Chicago Press, 1948), pp. xi-xii.

[147] Paul Tillich, **Systematic Theology**, Vol. I, **op.cit.**, p. 110.

[148] **Ibid.**, pp. 113, 186.

[149] Paul Tillich, **The Shaking of the Foundations, op.cit.**, p. 59.

[150] cf. S. Paul Schilling, **op.cit.**, p. 168.

148

[151] cf. John A. T. Robinson, **Honest to God** (Philadelphia: The Westminster Press, 1963), pp. 73-74.

[152] Paul Tillich, **Systematic Theology**, Vol. I, **op.cit.**, p. 148.

[153] **Ibid.**, pp. 6-9.

[154] **Ibid.**, p. 12.

[155] **Ibid.**, pp. 12-14.

[156] **Ibid.**, p. 15.

[157] **Ibid.**, p. 50.

[158] cf. L. Gordon Tait, **The Promise of Tillich** (Philadelphia: J. B. Lippincott Company, 1971), p. 37.

[159] cf. Paul Tillich, **Systematic Theology**, Vol. I, **op.cit.**, pp. 36-37.

[160] **Ibid.**, p. 60.

[161] cf. Tait, **op.cit.**, pp. 44-45.

[162] Nels F. S. Ferré, et al. **Paul Tillich: Retrospect and Future** (Nashville: Abingdon Press, 1966), p. 16.

[163] George H. Tavard, **Paul Tillich and the Christian Message** (New York: Charles Scribner's Sons, 1962), p. 167.

[164] Gerald O'Collins, S.J., "Interpreting Jesus Today," in **America** (October 1, 1983), pp. 165-168.

[165] cf. Paul Tillich, **Systematic Theology**, Vol. I, **op.cit.**, p. 235.

[166] **Ibid.**, p. 236.

[167] Paul Tillich, **The Shaking of the Foundations, op.cit.**, pp. 52-63. Cf. also John A. T. Robinson, **Honest To God** (Philadelphia: The Westminster Press, 1963), pp. 45-63.

[168] cf. Paul Tillich, **Dynamics of Faith** (New York: Harper and Row, 1957), pp. 41-54.

[169] cf. L. Gordon Tait, **op.cit.**, pp. 52-53.

[170] cf. Lee, **op.cit.**, pp. 209-54.

[171] John B. Cobb, Jr., **Christ in a Pluralistic Age** (Philadelphia: The Western Press, 1975).

[172] cf. Lewis S. Ford, in **Horizons**, Vol. 4, No. 2 (Fall, 1977), pp. 255-57.

[173] John B. Cobb, Jr., **Christ in a Pluralistic Age, op.cit., p. 187.**

[174] **Ibid.**, pp. 51, 187.

[175] **Ibid.**, p. 42.

[176] **Ibid.**, p. 24.

[177] **Ibid.**, p. 18.

[178] **Ibid.**, p. 24.

[179] **Ibid.**, p. 256.

[180] **Ibid.**, p. 17.

[181] **Ibid.**, pp. 170ff., 138.

[182] John B. Cobb, Jr., **Christ in a Pluralistic Age, op.cit.**, p. 171.

[183] **Ibid.**, p. 139.

[184] **Ibid.**, p. 140.

[185] cf. **Ibid.**, p. 142.

[186] **Ibid.**, p. 173.

[187] cf. **Ibid.**, pp. 22ff., 24, 177.

[188] John B. Cobb, Jr., "Response to Ogden and Carpenter," **op.cit.**, p. 125.

[189] cf. Robert E. Doud, "Rahner's Christology: A Whiteheadian Critique," **Journal of Religion** 57/2 (April, 1977), pp. 144-155.

[190] cf. Schubert M. Ogden, "Christology Reconsidered: John Cobb's 'Christ in a Pluralistic Age'," in **Process Studies**, Vol. 6, No. 2 (Summer, 1976), pp. 116-22.

[191] John B. Cobb. Jr., **Christ in a Pluralistic Age, op.cit.**, p. 261.

[192] **Ibid.**, p. 142.

[193] **Ibid.**, pp. 53, 51.

[194] **Ibid.**, pp. 19ff.

[195] **Ibid.**, p. 63.

[196] John B. Cobb, Jr., "Response to Ogden and Carpenter," **op.cit.**, p. 123.

[197] Schubert M. Ogden, "Christology Reconsidered: John Cobb's 'Christ in a Pluralistic Age'," **op.cit.**, p. 118.

[198] **Ibid.**, p. 118; cf. also John B. Cobb, in **op.cit.**, p. 85.

[199] **Ibid.**, p. 124.

[200] cf. John B. Cobb, Jr., **Christ in a Pluralistic Age. op.cit.**, pp. 136-176.

[201] Ogden, **op.cit.**, pp. 118-19; cf. also John B. Cobb, Jr., **Christ in a Pluralistic Age**, p. 17.

[202] cf. John B. Cobb, Jr., **op.cit.**, p. 54.

[203] Ogden, **op.cit.**, p. 119.

[204] John B. Cobb, Jr., **op.cit.**, p. 141.

[205] **Ibid.**, p. 138.

[206] **Ibid.**, p. 136.

[207] **Ibid.**, pp. 24-133.

[208] cf. Ogden, **op.cit.**, pp. 119-20.

[209] John B. Cobb, Jr., **Christ in a Pluralistic Age, op.cit.**, pp. 132-138.

[210] **Ibid.**, p. 101.

[211] Schubert M. Ogden, **op.cit.**, p. 120.

[212] John B. Cobb, Jr., **Christ in a Pluralistic Age, op.cit.**, p. 142.

[213] **Ibid.**, p. 173.

[214] cf. Ogden, **op.cit.**, p. 121.

[215] John B. Cobb, Jr., **Christ in a Pluralistic Age, op. cit.**, p. 142.

[216] Ogden, **op.cit.**, pp. 121-22.

[217] John B. Cobb, Jr., "Response to Ogden and Carpenter," **op.cit.**, p. 124.

[218] John B. Cobb, Jr., "Response to Ogden and Carpenter," **op.cit.**, p. 124.

[219] Ogden, **op.cit.**, p. 120.

[220] John B. Cobb, Jr., "Response to Ogden and Carpenter," **op.cit.**, p. 125.

[221] cf. Schubert M. Ogden, "The Point of Christology," in **The Journal of Religion,** 55/4 (October, 1975), pp. 375-95.

[222] John B. Cobb, Jr., "Response to Ogden and Carpenter," **op.cit.**, p. 126.

[223] cf. Bernard E. Meland, **Fallible Forms and Symbols** (Philadelphia: Fortress Press, 1976).

[224] cf. John B. Cobb, Jr., "Buddhist Emptiness and the Christian God," in **Journal of the American Academy of Religion,** 45/1 (March, 1977), pp. 11-25.

[225] **Ibid.**, pp. 11-25; cf. also John B. Cobb, Jr. and David Ray Griffin, **Process Theology: An Introductory Exposition** (Philadelphia: The Westminster Press, 1976), pp. 136-42.

[226] John B. Cobb, Jr., and David Ray Griffin, **op.cit.**, pp. 140-41.

[227] Paul Tillich, **Systematic Theology**, Vol. I., **op.cit.**, p. 163.

[228] L. Gordon Tait, **op.cit.**, p. 48.

[229] Paul Tillich, **Love, Power, and Justice** (New York: Oxford University Press, 1954), p. 19.

[230] cf. Tillich, **Systematic Theology**, Vol. I, **op.cit.**, pp. 164-168; pp. 168-174; pp. 174-186; pp. 188-189.

[231] Kenneth Hamilton, **The System and the Gospel** (New York: The Macmillan Company, 1963), p. 227.

[232] cf. Guyton B. Hammond, **The Power of Self-Transcendence** (St. Louis: The Bethany Press, 1966), p. 109.

[233] L. Gordon Tait, **op.cit.**, pp. 98-99.

[234] Paul Tillich, **Systematic Theology**, Vol. III, **op.cit.**, p. 4.

[235] cf. Nels F.S. Ferré, et al., **Paul Tillich: Retrospect and Future, op.cit.**, p. 7.

[236] cf. esp. J. Heywood Thomas, **Paul Tillich: An Appraisal** (Philadelphia: The Westminster Press, 1963); George H. Tavard, op.cit.; Kenneth Hamilton, **op.cit.**

[237] cf. Paul Tillich, **Systematic Theology, op.cit.**, Vol. II, p. 80.

[238] cf. Paul Tillich, **Ibid.**, pp. 29-78.

[239] Paul Tillich, **Systematic Theology**, Vol. II, **op.cit.**, p. 97.

[240] **Ibid.**, pp. 98-99.

[241] **Ibid.**, p. 101.

[242] **Ibid.**, p. 107.

[243] **Ibid.**, pp. 114-15.

[244] **Ibid.**, p. 94.

[245] Nels F. S. Ferré, "The Fabric of Paul Tillich's Theology," in **Scottish Journal of Theology**, Vol. 21, No. 2 (June, 1968), pp. 164-65.

[246] cf. Langdon Gilkey, **Naming The Whirlwind: The Renewal of God-Language** (Indianapolis: The Bobbs-Merrill Company, 1970), pp. 454-57.

[247] Robert N. Bellah, **Beyond Belief** (New York: Harper and Row, 1970), p. 245.

[248] cf. Paul Tillich, **Systematic Theology**, Vol. 2, **op.cit.**, pp. 87-88.

[249] **Ibid.**, p. 89.

[250] Paul Tillich, "On the Boundary Line," in **The Christian Century**, Vol. LXXVII, No. 49 (December 7, 1960), p. 1435.

[251] Paul Tillich, **Christianity and the Encounter of the World Religions** (New York: Columbia University Press, 1963), p. 64.

[252] L. Gordon Tait, **op.cit.**, pp. 107-08.

[253] cf. Bernard E. Meland, **Fallible Forms and Symbols: Discourses on Method in a Theology of Culture** (Philadelphia: Fortress Press, 1976), pp. 139ff.

[254] **Ibid.**

[255] **Ibid.**, p. 75.

[256] Paul Tillich, **Systematic Theology**, Vol. II, **op.cit.**, pp. 174-75.

[257] Ewert H. Cousins, "Process Models in Culture, Philosophy, and Theology," in **Process Theology: Basic Writings,** ed. by Ewert H. Cousins (New York: Newman Press, 1971), p. 20.

[258] Paul Tillich, Systematic Theology, Vol. II, **op.cit.**, p. 123; pp. 134-35.

[259] **Ibid.**, p. 144.

[260] **Ibid.**, p. 148.

[261] **Ibid.**, pp. 152-55.

[262] **Ibid.**, p. 170.

[263] **Ibid.**, pp. 174-76.

[264] Daniel Day Williams, "Suffering and Being in Empirical Theology," in **The Future of Empirical Theology**, ed. by Bernard Meland (Chicago: Chicago University Press, 1969), pp. 191-92.

[265] Alfred North Whitehead, **Process and Reality** (New York: Macmillan, 1929), p. 525.

[266] Samuel H. Beer, **The City of Reason** (Cambridge: Harvard University Press, 1949), p. 131.

[267] cf. Lewis S. Ford, "Divine Persuasion and the Triumph of Good," in **Philosophy of Religion: Contemporary Perspectives**, ed. by Norbert O. Schedler (New York: Macmillan Publishing Co., Inc., 1974), p. 493.

[268] Alfred North Whitehead, **Process and Reality, op.cit.**, p. 517.

[269] **Ibid.**, p. 531.

[270] George F. Thomas, **Religious Philosophies of The West** (New York: Charles Scribner's Sons, 1965), p. 389.

[271] cf. Alfred North Whitehead, **Process and Reality, op.cit.**, p. 33.

[272] **Ibid.**, p. 532.

[273] cf. Paul Tillich, **Systematic Theology**, Vol. II, **op.cit.**, pp. 114-15.

[274] Paul Tillich, **Systematic Theology**, Vol. I, **op.cit.**, p. 135.

[275] cf. Paul Tillich, **Systematic Theology**, Vol. I, **op.cit.**, p. 136.

[276] Alfred North Whitehead, **Process and Reality, op.cit.**, p. 256.

[277] Bernard J. Lee, "The Sacrament of Creative Transformation," in **Process Studies**, Vol. 8, No. 4 (Winter, 1978), p. 240.

[278] **Ibid.**, p. 241.

[279] cf. Alfred North Whitehead, **Process and Reality, op.cit.**, p. 187.

[280] Alfred North Whitehead, **Science and the Modern World** (New York: The Macmillan Company, 1925), p. 172.

[281] Bernard J. Lee, "The Sacrament of Creative Transformation," **op.cit.**, p. 243.

[282] William A. Beardslee, **A House for Hope** (Philadelphia: Westminster Press, 1972), p. 160.

[283] John B. Cobb, Jr., **Christ in a Pluralistic Age, op.cit.**, pp. 84ff; cf. passim.

[284] cf. Bernard J. Lee, "The Sacrament of Creative Transformation," **op.cit.**, pp. 243-44.

[285] cf. Clement of Alexandria, Stromateis, V, 13.

[286] Clement of Alexandria, Stromateis, I, 15.

[287] Augustine, **The Retractions**, I, 13.

[288] cf. Tyron Inbody, "Paul Tillich and Process Theology," in **Theological Studies**, Vol. 36, No. 3 (September 1975), p. 492.

[289] Cyprian Cooney, **Understanding the New Theology** (Milwaukee: Bruce Publishing Company, 1969), pp. 54-55.

[290] Edward Schillebeeckx, **God: The Future of Man** (New York: Sheed and Ward, 1968), p. 77.

[291] Piet Schoonenberg, **The Christ** (New York: Herder and Herder, 1971), p. 73.

[292] Donald P. Gray, **Jesus: The Way to Freedom** (Winona: Saint Mary's Press, 1979), p. 67.

[293] cf. Richard H. Niebuhr, **The Meaning of Revelation** (New York: Macmillan Paperbacks, 1960), p. 68.

[294] Jung Young Lee, **God Suffers For Us: A Systematic Inquiry into the Concept of Divine Passibility** (The Hague: Martinus Nijhoff, 1974), p. 1.

[295] Warren McWilliams, "Daniel Day Williams' Vulnerable and Invulnerable God," in **Encounter** (Winter, 1982), p. 74.

[296] Daniel Day Williams, "The Vulnerable and the Invulnerable God," in **Christianity and Crisis**, Vol. 22 (March 5, 1962), p. 27.

[297] **Ibid.**, p. 28.

[298] Daniel Day Williams, **The Spirit and the Forms of Love** (New York: Harper & Row, 1968), p. 166.

[299] Williams, **The Spirit and the Forms of Love**, p. 167.

[300] **Ibid.**, p. 184.

[301] **Ibid.**, p. 185.

[302] Daniel Day Williams, "Suffering and Being in Empirical Theology," in Bernard E. Meland (ed.), **The Future of Empirical Theology** (Chicago: University of Chicago Press, 1969), p. 192.

[303] Daniel Day Williams, **What Present Day Theologians are Thinking** , 3rd ed. (New York: Harper & Row, 1967), p. 172.

[304] cf. Warren McWilliams, "Daniel Day Williams' Vulnerable and Invulnerable God," **op.cit.**, p. 89.

[305] John Shea, **The God Who Fell From Heaven** (Niles, Ill.: Argus Commmunications, 1979), p. 90.

Blasi, Anthony J.

A PHENOMENOLOGICAL TRANSFORMATION OF THE SOCIAL SCIENTIFIC STUDY OF RELIGION

American University Studies: Series 7, Theology and Religion, Vol. 10
ISBN 0-8204-0235-4   205 pp.   hardback US $ 27.85

Recommended prices - alterations reserved

This book develops a theoretical methodology for the scientific study of religion, from the principle of meaning adequacy. Religion is to be understood adequately when the character of its presence in the mind of the religious person is described. This methodology is used to address some major issues in the study of religion in new ways – defining religion, understanding ritual, the connection between religion and morality, religious social morality in the third world, pietism, the value problem in scientific accounts of religion, and types of religious mentalities. These discussions comprise a substantive phenomenology of religion, and a distinctive sociology of religion.

Contents: After developing a phenomenological methodology for the study of religion, the book addresses major issues in the social scientific study of religion. Among these are ritual, morality, and conversion.

PETER LANG PUBLISHING, INC.
62 West 45th Street
USA – New York, NY 10036

Herbert W. Basser

MIDRASHIC INTERPRETATIONS OF
THE SONG OF MOSES

American University Studies: Series VII, Theology and Religion. Vol. 2
ISBN 0-8204-0065-3   326 p.   paperback US $ 28.85*

*Recommended price - alterations reserved

This work provides a translation of, and a commentary to the text of *Sifre Ha'azinu*. Finkelstein's edition (1939, reprinted JTS 1969) and selected readings of the London manuscript of this midrash appear in translation with full notes covering textual observations, philological inquiries and exegetical problems. The following ideas are discussed within the course of the work: midrashic forms, the use of Scripture in midrash, the dating of the traditions and of the recording of this midrash, the use of apologetic and polemic in midrash. An *Introduction* and *Conclusion* have been provided which discuss the items in this midrash which are relevant to the academic study of Judaism. The literary aspects of this midrash on Deut. 32 are used to exemplify *midrashim* on poetic Scriptures.

Contents: Introduction discussing literary, theological, historical aspects of midrash - Translation and analysis of the midrash to Deut. 32. Sifre Deuteronomy - Conclusion summing up the findings in the work.

PETER LANG PUBLISHING, INC.
62 West 45th Street
USA - New York, NY 10036